My Life
with Roger

*Celebrating Forty-Plus Years
of Laughter, Travel and Sports*

by
Rosemarie Olhausen

Shapato Publishing, LLC
Everly, Iowa

Published by: Shapato Publishing
PO Box 476
Everly, IA 51338

ISBN: 978-0-9833526-4-8

Library of Congress Control Number: 2011928366
Copyright © 2011 Rosemarie Olhausen

All rights reserved. No part of this book may be reproduced or transmitted in any form or by any means, electronic or mechanical, including photocopying, recording, or by an information storage and retrieval system, without permission in writing from the publisher.

First Printing May 2011

Additional editing by Colleen O'Brien Clopton

To Roger, who continues to make each day an adventure and keeps me on my toes, wondering what fun is yet to come.

Thanks for letting me do crazy things, like write a book about our life together.

PREFACE

Almost 20 years ago a friend suggested I write a book about life with my husband, Roger. The only catch was that she thought I should just sell it as fiction because she didn't think people would ever believe that the stories were true. At the time I laughed it off because it had never occurred to me that I would be able to write a book. Now, after more than forty funny years of marriage, there seems to be plenty of material.

TABLE OF CONTENTS

ONE	*Dating and Biscuit Trails*	11
TWO	*Sheep Calls from the Bathroom*	19
THREE	*Getting to Know You*	35
FOUR	*Sink or Swim*	39
FIVE	*To Have or Not to Have*	43
SIX	*Teaching: Pop or Beer?*	55
SEVEN	*Coaching*	61
EIGHT	*Farmer Roger*	73
NINE	*The Growing Years*	83
TEN	*Mr. Little League*	89
ELEVEN	*Entering the Twenty-First Century*	93
TWELVE	*On the Road Again*	99
THIRTEEN	*I Had a Dream*	113
FOURTEEN	*I Might Need That – Boxes and Boxes*	115

FIFTEEN	*Where's Waldo?*	121
SIXTEEN	*Kum & Go Ties / This Old Hat*	125
SEVENTEEN	*It's a Secret*	129
EIGHTEEN	*The Next Stage – Retirement*	133
NINETEEN	*If I Had Known*	145
TWENTY	*Happily Ever After*	149

My Life
with Roger

*Celebrating Forty-Plus Years
of Laughter, Travel and Sports*

ONE

Dating and Biscuit Trails

It all began after I got my first teaching job. It was 1967 and I was hired to teach middle school home economics in Jefferson, Iowa.

That spring, my mother and I made a trip to Jefferson so I could look over my new classroom and prepare to move to town. While we were at the school, one of the veteran teachers, Ray Dillard, stopped to introduce himself. He thought my mother was the new teacher.

I was miffed he hadn't recognized that I would be the new teacher as I was dressed in a cotton floral suit, which, after all, was the latest style, and I thought I looked very much like a teacher.

After scouting out my classroom, Mom and I were off to find suitable housing.

The first building that we thought must surely be apartments turned out to be Slininger Funeral Home, so we decided to ask for help in finding a place before we embarrassed ourselves further.

Finding nothing to rent, we took a break and went out for lunch at the truck stop, which in the day was about the only place to eat. We were seated in a booth, enjoying our lunch and talking about our day when four men walked by and sat across the aisle a couple of booths away. I was facing that way and recognized one of them as Mr. Dillard, the teacher we had met earlier.

Evidently he recognized me too—it must have been the suit!—as moments later all four heads leaned to the center of the table while he told them something. Then, in unison, all turned and looked at me.

Little did I know that in a little more than a year, I would be married to the eighth grade math teacher who'd turned and looked at me.

My excitement that day was that I ended up renting a small, two-bedroom house and was thrilled to have a home of my own.

Later, I would get all excited about that math teacher.

~ ~ ~

I graduated from Iowa State University at the end of summer school. The ceremony was held in the morning and that afternoon there was a seventh-grade introductory day at my new school in Jefferson.

As I got to my classroom and was trying to look prepared—I didn't even know what I was supposed to be telling them—the eighth-grade math teacher stopped in to introduce himself. Making an impression on him was the last thing on my mind. But we made some talk before he went on his way and I introduced myself to the new seventh graders.

As the school year got under way, the long-time guidance counselor told me that she had counseled the former home economics teacher to find a different job because she had a huge crush on that math teacher. I decided then and there that I would not show any interest in him, and for a while I would actually walk down the halls without speaking to him.

However, that didn't last long. Soon I was chatting with him and he was coming by my classroom more and more often, even though his classroom was on the floor below.

In the layout of the middle school, the main stairs sat across the hall from my classroom. On one side of the stairs was the principal's office, and on the other side was the mimeograph room where teachers made copies of worksheets and tests.

During the fall I taught an adult sewing class one evening a week. I noticed that Roger seemed to copy his students' worksheets during that time, and seemed to finish about the time the sewing class was over. We would chat for a short time at first, but eventually we talked at greater length.

One evening I was working at school when he dropped in after making copies. My seventh-grade girls had had a lesson on making biscuits, and that day each of the six kitchens in all four classes had made biscuits. Being a first-year teacher, I had not thought ahead to how many biscuits would be produced if I did not cut the recipe in half, so there were mounds of biscuits in each kitchen.

Roger and I decided we really should get rid of the biscuits, so we sacked them up and took them with us.

Off we went in his car with dozens of biscuits and no plan. We ended up going to the trailer court where some teacher friends lived, and throwing biscuits at their trailer. They never checked outside, so we decided they hadn't heard us.

Still having lots of biscuits left and not really wanting to part company yet, we just drove around and eventually started down Highway 30 to the east.

Out in the country was a small café where Roger said he'd treat me to a snack. He decided he wanted peaches with cream.

(Mind you, I hated peaches. In second grade I would fake a stomach ache each day peaches were to be served at school lunch because we had to eat everything on our plates and peaches made me gag.

My mother and the teacher soon got on to what I was doing, so my ruse only worked for a short time.)

Wanting to make a good impression on Roger, I ordered the same thing he had. I must have been hanging on his every word, because the peaches and cream went down without one gagging sound coming from my mouth. I just smiled and ate them. It's amazing what one is capable of when one is falling in love.

After our snack, we figured that as long as we were that close to Ogden we would leave a trail of biscuits for the elderly lady who drove from there to teach seventh-grade English in our building.

She arrived safely the next day but didn't mention anything about the trail we'd marked. However, I had a really hard time keeping a straight face when the teacher from the trailer court came and told me that some of the students must have taken home a lot of biscuits because they were all over his yard.

It was even funnier when they cleaned off the top of the trailer in the spring and found more biscuits up there.

We never told.

~ ~ ~

Roger didn't ask me out on any real dates for several months, but we had fun doing impromptu things like playing "fox and geese" in the fresh snow by the new high school. I don't remember being cold while making the tracks, even though I was wearing open-toed, sling-back shoes.

The first day of Christmas break, I ran up town to quickly pick up something, and ran into Roger. He thought I looked fine, even though I had on old clothes and no makeup, and he convinced me to go to Ames with him.

We had a fun day shopping and goofing around, but I got back only an hour before my family and some friends were to arrive for supper. I'd spent the entire day thinking of Roger instead of the meal I was supposed to be preparing.

Not being an experienced hostess, I had to think fast. I decided on chili, and my brother will never let me forget how they drove 40 miles for a bowl of chili—and I'd had to call and have them bring more bowls.

Roger finally asked me for a date on Saturday, January 13, 1968.

He took me on a typical '60s date—pizza and a movie. We went to Ames, and on the way there we talked about all the things we wanted to do. They were almost all the same things. Roger said we'd have to be together for years to get it all done.

I looked at him and replied that I didn't intend to spend years dating anyone.

Roger said, "Then maybe we should get married."

Not knowing him really well, but liking him a lot, I said, "Okay."

That's when he told me he would give me a week to think about it, and he would ask me every day during that week.

I still wasn't sure he was serious. I had talked about marriage with a couple other guys in the same light-hearted manner, and obviously nothing had come of those talks.

The following week was exhilarating because each day he did ask me in a different way. One morning before school he showed up at my little house and left candy and a note. Other days I would find a note on my desk when I arrived at school, or he would stop in my classroom before the students arrived.

The next Saturday night we went to Ames for pizza and a movie. We saw Clint Eastwood's The Good, the Bad and the Ugly, a real guy's western.

But at the appointed time of 9 p.m., which was my last chance to say "no" to the proposal, we left the movie and stepped out on the sidewalk, where Roger proposed one last time. When I said "yes," it was a done deal and sealed with a kiss . . . right there on Main Street on January 20, 1968.

~ ~ ~

Over the next few weeks I learned more about Roger through the notes he left on my desk each day. He would arrive at school before I did, and when I entered my room I'd find notes about his family and childhood.

All the notes were addressed to "Miss L" or "Miss Love," as that's what he called me then. I thought it was quite romantic, but I imagine it was in part because he couldn't always remember my name.

While we were dating, and for the first couple of years after we were married, I was instructed that if we met someone I didn't know, I was to just walk away so he didn't have to introduce me. That should have been my first clue that I was marrying an absent-minded professor type, but it didn't make any difference. I was in love.

TWO

Sheep Calls from the Bathroom

What a courtship we had. Roger was shy about being with me in Jefferson, as the middle and high school kids would see us, so most of our dating was out of town.

But gas was cheap then and we thought nothing of going to Ames or Des Moines for an evening. Little did I know that jumping in the car to go anywhere at any time would be the norm of our lives.

Although it would be months before I met Roger's family, we did stop at my folks' farm, so he got acquainted with my family.

Having come from a family where he was the youngest of three boys, Roger was a little out of his league when he met my two sisters. The first time we stopped at my family's, we were returning to Jefferson from Des Moines, and it was getting close to my sisters' bedtime. My sisters Jeannie and Phyllis are a few years younger than I am. At twelve and fourteen at the time, they weren't old enough to be dating, but were always interested in checking out my boyfriends.

They came downstairs to see us, both dressed in their long, flannel nightgowns, robes, crazy slippers, their hair in big rollers and "bump gunk"—also know as Clearasil—on their faces. Roger didn't know what to think of them as they giggled and acted like the 12- and 14-year-olds they were.

As we continued to date, we stopped several times to visit my family, and although my college-age brother, Glenn, and my sisters liked Rog, they *really* liked to tease me.

In the past they'd always found something about my boyfriends to make fun of, and as soon as these cattle-farm-raised kids found out that Roger's family had raised sheep, that became their area of concentration.

While Roger and I visited with my parents, my siblings would leave the room one or two at a time and from the kitchen or downstairs bathroom I would hear "Baaa, baaa."

He never reacted. It wasn't until he'd been in the family for several years—and they had grown up!—that they confessed to doing this. Roger said, "I guess I was so nervous that I never heard them."

One of the stories that my family likes best about getting to know Roger was the evening we stopped to visit and Mom served one of her special desserts. It was a frozen treat with lots of goodies that included small colored marshmallows, peanuts and chocolate chips, all in ice cream. Wanting to compliment the cook, Roger said how good it was and commented about all the extra things he was finding. When he said something about its even having bubblegum in it, we all looked at each other before Mom said that wasn't one of the ingredients.

With an embarrassed look, Roger said, "Oh, I was chewing bubblegum and put it on the side of my plate before I started eating and must have gotten it in with one bite."

Ever since that night we've called it our Bubblegum Dessert.

Most of our dates were nothing fancy, although we did go to a couple of concerts. Probably our favorite was The Lettermen. Afterwards we got an eight-track tape of their songs and drove around playing "Going Out Of My Head Over You" and "Spooky."

One Sunday, as I was preparing for a date with Roger, he called. He had organized a men's basketball league that played on Sundays in the gym of the nearby small town of Cooper. That particular day one of the men had gotten really mad about something and taken it out on Roger, telling him to stay out of Cooper.

Rog told me he wouldn't be picking me up for our date. He then gave the phone to a woman who I didn't know, and had her talk to me. She confirmed there had been a problem, but since we were unacquainted, we didn't have much to say to each other and I didn't get any details.

Thinking Roger had been kidding, I continued to primp for the date. I got dressed and waited.

And waited.

I finally called the teacher Roger roomed with and found that he'd gone to Ames alone. I couldn't believe it.

Later I learned that this wasn't the first time he'd done something similar. When he was the team quarterback in high school and they lost their homecoming game he'd been so upset that he just didn't go pick up his date for the dance. She didn't take it well and never went out with him again.

At least I had gotten notice. I just hadn't believed it.

~ ~ ~

Every once in a while I still hear stories about when Roger was growing up in Hartley. Some of my favorite stories took place when he was in kindergarten.

After the first day of school, he surprised his mother by telling her he knew who he would marry some day. When she asked him who the lucky girl would be, he replied, "Barbara Olhausen."

Upon further questioning, he told his mother that he'd decided this because they both had the same last name and that would make it easier than marrying someone with a different last name.

Very logical, for a kindergartner.

At that time school pictures were simply a class picture. While riding the bus home from school with his new kindergarten class picture, he took his pencil and poked the eyes out of everyone in the picture.

Needless to say, his mother wasn't happy about that. The next year, when it was time for the pictures to be brought home, she impressed on him that it was important to take good care of this picture and not to poke out eyes or do anything else to damage it.

Being mindful of what his mother said, he carefully folded it up into a small square and put it in his pocket. He still has the class picture where he poked out the eyes, but she must have decided the other was beyond saving, as he doesn't have it.

One source of anxiety while Roger was growing up was May Day. He dreaded this day because his mother would make him take May baskets to the little girls in his class.

The practice was that when a May basket was delivered, the recipient would chase down the person delivering it and kiss them. The thought of this traumatized little Roger and he would cry and cry about having to do it. Nevertheless, his mother, Leona, would make the May baskets and drive him around to the girls' homes.

Roger remembers knocking on the doors, setting the baskets down and running as fast as he could to the car. Once in the car he would hide down on the floor while his mother waved to the young girls who were looking for him.

The Olhausen boys were quite the athletes. From the time the oldest, Cloy, was a freshman, until Roger graduated, the football team was quarterbacked by an Olhausen.

With Cloy six years older than Roger and Dale four years older than Roger, that made a run of about 10 years, all with impressive winning seasons. Cloy was not only the oldest, but the largest of the brothers, and Roger was not big enough to intimidate anyone. When he was a senior he was only 5-feet-6-inches tall, but very athletic. The following article from the Des Moines Register was given to Roger by an aunt when she was older and cleaning out some things from her house.

Ever heard of Roger Olhausen?

He's Hartley's fullback—and speaking of pound-for-pound Roger's doing all right.

Take, for example, the other night when the young Hawks lost a narrow 14-13 decision to Milford.

Olhausen pitched a 23-yard scoring pass to Norman Kerney early and later in the game Roger connected on a 50-yard gainer via the airplanes to end Bob Feddersen.

Working out of the Hartley single wing against the Pioneers, Olhausen completed four out of seven aerial attempts for a total of 110 yards.

Perhaps only penalties kept the Hawks from winning that one as Olhausen keyed most of his mates' drives. Roger's efforts were quite respectable, especially in view of an injury he suffered a short time before last week's duel with Milford.

A tractor wheel backed over his foot at the Olhausen farm and all Roger could do against Milford was spin, take a step and – throw that pigskin. Which he did very well. Olhausen has fired five touch-down passes this fall for the Hawks.

And before the season beckons goodbye, Roger should have several more, even though: He weighs only 118 pounds dripping wet.

Roger is still proud of the time he went to state track meet on a relay team. I don't remember how they did, but it was a high point for him. Only once have I heard him talk about playing baseball. He only played his freshman year because the baseball and track seasons overlapped and track was his favorite. Roger was a pitcher, and in one game made all of the outs. He either struck them out, caught the hit ball or threw the runner out.

Amazing. And he would rather run around a track.

~ ~ ~

As the school year came to a close, our romance was in full swing. Roger and I were caught by the principal several times talking after the bell had rung for the beginning of class. He must have been a romantic, as he never said a word.

My ninth-grade girls seemed to think we were a good match and worked to get us together. Daily they would bring me messages from his room downstairs.

"Mr. Olhausen thinks you're cute."

"Mr. Olhausen said to tell you Hi."

I was never sure if he'd really told them to tell me or if they were just making it up. He did have them bring me notes on occasion, and I would have to come up with a reason that he was calling me "Miss L."

I don't think either of us got anything done during that last study hall.

One evening while talking on the phone with me, Rog must have been especially distracted because the next morning he couldn't find his school keys. After searching and searching with no luck, he came to the conclusion that he must have dropped them into the wastebasket, which had then been dumped into the garbage, which had already been picked up that morning.

He stopped in my room before school to tell me what he'd done and said that he was going to get permission to skip the teachers' meeting after school to go to the dump and look for his keys.

Being head-over-heels in love with him, I decided two sets of eyes would be better than one, so I also got permission to go to the dump after school instead of staying for the teachers' meeting.

Not knowing where the garbage had been dumped, we had little chance of finding the keys and just wandered around for a while before deciding it was a lost cause.

The lost keys should have been another clue to the fact that Roger might be an absent-minded professor, but it never crossed my mind . . . then.

~ ~ ~

With the end of the school year approaching, we still talked marriage occasionally but had not set a date or even become officially engaged.

Being a first-year teacher was stressful, and as a home economics teacher I had many special projects going on. The two ninth-grade classes were finishing the year with a unit on sewing, and I was told we needed to have a style show at the end of the year.

Great.

Some of the students didn't have an aptitude for sewing, and I spent many hours after the school day was over helping them. A few articles of clothing still weren't done for the style show, but thanks to my college roommate, I knew what to do.

We stapled and taped.

The last few days were a panic trying to get everyone's projects done and I was seeing less of Roger. With only one day of school left, I had to have help. I asked my mother and sisters to help me grade the projects so the students could take them home on the last day.

I evaluated the projects while my mom and sisters wrote down the comments and grades. We worked into the evening, ate sandwiches in my classroom, and after they left, I went home tired.

But not too tired to see Roger.

He came over and we visited, but finally I hinted that it might be time for him to leave. In his own unique way, he handed me a box and said, "Do you want this?"

Inside was the ring!

I said, "Yes!"

He confessed he'd had it for a while and couldn't decide when to give it to me, but finally decided that I should have it for the last day of school so all our students could see it.

A group of ninth-grade girls usually came to visit with me as I stood outside my room on hall duty every morning. On that particular morning I didn't say anything about being engaged, but just waved my left hand around as I talked . . . until finally they noticed my new ring.

What excitement we caused! They not only wanted to talk to Mr. O about it, they stood in line at the student phone in the hall to call their mothers and tell them.

(Remember, this was 1968, when mothers stayed at home and cell phones were still 30 years in the future.)

One teacher even let her homeroom out so they could all file past me and see my engagement ring.

~ ~ ~

I first met the Olhausen family on Mother's Day.

After Roger taught Sunday school that day we drove to Hartley for dinner with his folks. I was nervous, but all went well and we even went over to his brother's house to meet Cloy and his wife, Connie.

On our way back home, Roger told me that I would be the largest of the sister-in-laws.

I was speechless over this unbelievable statement because I was an average size and didn't think they were much smaller.

Much later his mother told me that he had written to them about me, so she knew we were serious. Both of his brothers had married hometown girls they had known all their lives, so this was a new experience for their family, too.

Since it was so late the night we got engaged, I hadn't even called my parents to tell them the good news. Several weeks earlier I'd shown them a cartoon of a little girl coming home and saying that she was going to marry a boy named Roger, but I don't think they thought I was serious.

After school that day we drove to Dallas Center to tell my folks. When we arrived my dad was mowing the lawn and Mom was preparing a picnic supper.

They were glad to see us and asked us to stay. Then Roger told them that we were engaged. A moment of silence followed, after which my dad muttered he had to do chores, turned and left, and my brother Glenn followed.

Mom and the girls were excited and wanted to see my ring.

Rog decided to finish the mowing.

Mom, my sisters and I went inside to finish supper. I remember Mom pacing around wondering what to fix to eat. I pointed out that she already had everything set out for the picnic in the yard, so our engagement supper consisted of hotdogs and chips with toasted marshmallows for dessert.

Everyone was flustered and excited and didn't really know how to act. But I think everyone was happy—even if his family had been sheep farmers.

~ ~ ~

On Memorial Day the Olhausens always went to Lake Okoboji for a picnic and fishing, so we went up to meet them there. My family had never lived around water or vacationed at lakes. We were more likely to go to Wyoming. I'd never been fishing, didn't like worms and wasn't about to touch anything concerned with fish.

That said, I'm not sure how the day went, but know Roger didn't require me to bait the hooks. The only part that I remember vividly was that we met his family at a bait shack where they were purchasing worms. That's where Roger told them we were engaged.

Not the way I'd pictured our engagement being announced.

Now that school was out, we had time to think about a wedding. In 1968 a wedding wasn't as big a deal as it is today and didn't take as much planning.

The date was set for Saturday, July 13, since his brother and family from Colorado would be back for the fourth of July and could stay that long.

Note: This would be exactly six months after Roger asked me to marry him and only about a month and a half after we got engaged. He seemed shy, but he acted fast.

In the days before wedding planners, we had one. Roger and I were rather oblivious to everything, and thankfully my mother made sure we got things done. She did much more than I realized until later.

Meanwhile, Roger and I were just enjoying the summer and being in love.

We were to live in the small house that he rented, and since the place I'd been living was completely furnished I didn't have anything to bring into the home except a gold chair from my grandparents and a wonderfully long (7-foot) green couch that my parents gave us as a wedding present.

The only thing Roger and I purchased as we started our life together was a blue Pontiac Lemans convertible that we bought shortly before the wedding.

Roger has always been a private person and didn't really want to invite anyone from Jefferson to the wedding. One of his friends sang, and the other couple who came from Jefferson invited themselves. A friend that he had stood up with earlier in the summer called to ask when and where the wedding was because they hadn't gotten their invitation yet. In reality it hadn't even been sent, nor did we plan to send them one. We didn't even have an engagement announcement or wedding write-up in the Jefferson Bee and Herald. Most of our guests were relatives and friends of my family.

Now, as I think back, I wonder if he was shy about inviting friends, embarrassed to be marrying me, or what.

July 13, 1968 was an extremely warm day in Dallas Center, Iowa. The wedding was a late afternoon affair, so we couldn't have picked a hotter time. And, of course, this was before anyone even thought of having air conditioning in a church.

With the temperature close to 100 degrees, it was amazing that no one fainted. The minister was my old Sunday school teacher who was almost blind and deaf, but all went well. Only when he pronounced us man and wife and told Roger he could kiss his bride, did I realize how hot it really was.

I turned to face Rog for the kiss and he said, "Are you sure you want to do this?"

Then I noticed he was so hot that sweat was dripping off his chin, nose and eyebrows, and running from his forehead down his face.

Once again, love won out and I said, "Sure." I swear my makeup dropped a half inch after meeting up with his soaked face.

Since this was way before the days of fancy weddings, we had our reception in the church basement. The usual reception consisted of cake, mints, nuts and punch.

Because the Olhausen side had more than a three-hour drive home, my mother, sisters, friends and I had made a fresh fruit salad and sandwiches to add to that. After eating, opening gifts and accepting best wishes from all in attendance, we rode off in our new convertible with the usual tin cans behind us and with soap and shaving cream all over the car.

We stayed in Ames, at the Holiday Inn with a pool! Fancy! However, our excitement was somewhat dampered the next day when Rog went to wash the car and found that some of the paint was ruined because of the shaving cream.

~ ~ ~

As I look back, I laugh at some of our honeymoon. Sunday, upon leaving Ames, we went to Jefferson for a short time and Roger had me write some of our thank-you notes before continuing the honeymoon. I may be the only bride that wrote thank-you notes on the first day of her honeymoon.

Later in the afternoon we went to Clear Lake for a couple of days and one day drove to Minneapolis for a Minnesota Twins game.

But the funniest part was our stay in Clear Lake. While trying to be romantic, Roger wanted our motel room to be facing the lake. To this day he does not understand bed sizes and since he knew there would be two of us, he requested twin beds. He was astounded upon check-out when he commented that it was a great place to stay for a honeymoon and the owner said, "If I'd known you'd just gotten married you could have stayed in the honeymoon suite."

THREE

Getting to Know You

I understand from talk shows and articles in women's magazines that getting married and learning to live with someone is not without its trials, and that was certainly true of our experience.

Roger passed with flying colors on all the things I'd heard that men do that drive women crazy. He didn't leave the toilet seat up or the cap off the toothpaste. However, I'd never heard of someone hiding the mayonnaise.

That is the one food that Roger dislikes so much that he used to tell my younger sisters that they shouldn't eat it because it gave you cancer. Any time I had it out for a recipe or to put on my BLT, the moment I turned my back the jar would disappear.

Our house, and especially the kitchen, was small, but Rog kept me hopping trying to find the latest hiding place, whether it was behind the curtains, stashed in another room or even put in the trash. It didn't take me long to learn that Miracle Whip was treated the same way and I realized I would have to disguise the jar.

I will say that in our 42 years of marriage I can only recall one time that I made something that Roger wouldn't eat. Of course there were recipes that we decided were not worth repeating, but the one thing neither of us could eat was lamb stew.

Really bad.

Since then I've stuck with lamb burgers and lamb chops, before they started costing a dollar a bite.

Having grown up in a family of Democrats, marrying a strong Republican was trying. Being young and in love, when he convinced me that I should become a Republican, I agreed, as politics were of little interest to me.

I am glad that he took my word that I would do that and didn't have it written into the wedding vows as he'd first suggested. However, when we registered to vote for the first time after we married, he wouldn't go into the voting booth until he had heard me declare that I wanted to register as a Republican.

Another strong bone of contention was that I was an Iowa State fan. I had graduated from there just a year before and never thought it would be a problem in my marriage. Indeed, I was proud that I was a home economics teacher from there, as that occupation has very low divorce rate and ISU was ranked highly for the strong education department in that area.

However, Roger was and is a diehard Iowa Hawkeye fan.

Since I was not a huge sports fan, I mainly cheered for the Cyclones just to see his reaction. Anyone knowing him was surprised to hear that he spent his first year in college at ISU. Almost our entire marriage we've had season tickets for the Hawkeye football games. One of the first years of our marriage we were at an ISU vs. UI football game and I was standing and cheering for the Cyclones and Roger was standing and cheering for the Hawks when someone behind us leaned down to ask how long we'd been married because they weren't sure it would last if we were cheering for different teams.

But the year he offered to buy me season tickets in Ames while he would be getting his in Iowa City was the year I decided it was more fun to be with him than to cheer alone for my team.

Now our children and grandchildren are avid Hawkeye fans and we enjoy cheering together, so I think I made the right choice.

FOUR

Sink or Swim

One of Roger's best-kept secrets was that for his freshman year of college he attended Iowa State. His middle brother had convinced him that would be a good place to go to become an engineer, which would have been fine if that was what he had wanted to do.

Growing up, Roger had three careers he considered. The first was farming, since he'd grown up on a farm and enjoyed almost everything about it. However, he once had allergy tests and found that he was allergic to just about everything on a farm, so he decided against that.

Another choice was to become a minister. He has a deep faith but decided to put that one on the back burner and maybe do it as a second career. We have talked about it several times, and he was waiting to retire from teaching to return to school to become a pastor. After retiring, he did take several lay pastor classes but is just so busy he hasn't finished yet.

Teaching, his other choice, was the career path he chose. So after his freshman year in college, he transferred to Iowa Teachers College, which later became UNI.

All went well. He student-taught in Fort Dodge under Darrold Mohr, who would later become his principal. When Roger graduated, he was offered a job in Jefferson.

Roger was preparing for the beginning of the school year when the county superintendent called him a couple of days before school and said he hadn't received Rog's diploma, and did Roger have any idea what the problem could be?

Not wanting to admit it, but knowing what the holdup was, Roger said he'd check into it.

It seems that in days of yore it was required for all teachers to take a swimming class and pass it. Roger had taken the class during his freshman year at ISU. Coming from a working dairy farm had not left time for swimming lessons as a youth, so Roger wasn't too experienced in the pool. It seems that when the college swimming class started, Roger could do more than an adequate job for a while and was in the advanced group. But as the class advanced, Roger didn't. And when it came time to learn to swim on his back, he sank like a rock and was sent back to the lowest group.

Eventually everyone else advanced and he was left by himself.

After spending several class periods watching the same sinking routine, the teacher, wrestling coach Harold Nickols, hollered, "Forget it, Olhausen. You'll never learn to swim on your back! Just come up here with everyone else."

Because he couldn't swim on his back, he didn't get credit for the class. Now this had come back to haunt him, as he couldn't get his diploma without the swimming class.

To rectify this situation, Roger went to UNI, explained his problem that the swimming class hadn't transferred—without elaborating on his lack of ability to swim on his back—and got one of the powers-that-be to watch him swim.

This time he was not asked to do different strokes, and after watching him swim across the pool, the teacher said, "Well, you can swim," signed off on the class and Roger was able to start his first teaching job.

That's how close hundreds of students came to not having him as their teacher . . . a job he loved and did extremely well at for more than four decades.

The stories abound of Roger teaching and coaching, but that's for another chapter or two.

FIVE

To Have or Not to Have

Married life was good. Roger and I loved jumping into our blue convertible and going places. In those days we didn't go to all the Jefferson ballgames, like we do now, but also went to concerts, plays, out to eat, visited family and anything else that struck our fancy.

On July 20, 1969, shortly after our first anniversary, we were in Oregon watching Neil Armstrong walk on the moon. Although Roger had his master's degree before we started dating, he wanted to get a few more credits and we decided to make it a vacation as well as an educational experience.

We drove through Colorado to visit his brother and family on the way out but didn't tarry long anywhere. Arriving in the land of the University of Oregon Ducks in time to watch the moon walk, we then headed to student housing where we would spend the weeks Rog had class. Our temporary home was sparsely furnished, and we had only packed the basics—bedding, towels, clothes and a few pans. It was a great adventure. Most weekends we would journey to Portland to stay with Roger's aunt and uncle and enjoy the luxury of a real home.

While Roger was away at class, I was left to entertain myself. Realizing that I was quickly becoming bored, he found a fabric shop where he could drop me off on his way to class.

Long story made short, it was something new in the sewing world—all the fabrics were knits. I started taking classes while he was, and we ended up buying a new sewing machine and filling the car with fabric to take home to start a fabric shop in which I would teach. This ended up being the first business we would own, but only one of the many times Roger would indulge me in one of my wild dreams.

~ ~ ~

Although ours was a fast courtship, we had had some serious talks about our future. Good thing, since this was in the days before marriage counselors. Both of us had a strong desire to have a family sometime and had gone so far as to decide that if we couldn't have children of our own, we would adopt. Although we still planned to do that, we were having too good a time together to act on those plans. I enjoyed teaching home economics by day and sewing at night, and he was coaching three sports along with teaching his eighth grade math.

During the third year of our marriage we decided it was time to start a family. Having grown up as the youngest of three boys, Roger had never been around babies and was really wishing we could have kids and send them away for a couple years until they were potty trained and old enough to play.

At the end of my third year teaching, I resigned to stay home with our soon-to-be baby. Our son was born on October 21, 1970, and life got even better.

More than a year before our son's birth, Roger and I took two other couples to Minneapolis to watch a baseball game of his beloved Minnesota Twins. He had hyped the excitement that was to be had at the Twins stadium watching his favorite player, Harmon Killebrew, and was disappointed that we witnessed an unexciting, low-scoring game. However, his fondness for this team he'd rooted for as a young boy was not diminished, and our friends gave him a hard time about being such a devoted fan.

Before giving birth, we had found some cute baseball baby announcements and bought them in case we had a boy. Now Roger had a great idea and decided to act on it early the next morning. He took one of the announcements and wrote it out.

Before school he showed up at our friends' trailer home and gave them the announcement saying that we had named our first born Harmon Killebrew Olhausen.

Knowing how much Roger thought of this baseball player, our friend went to school and told everyone that was the baby's name. In reality the name was Randy Roger Olhausen. Roger got the last laugh this time.

When teachers have children it's often hard to come up with a name for a variety of reasons. We want a name that is easy to spell and pronounce, one that clearly lets you know what sex the child is, doesn't have initials that spell something funny, doesn't lend itself to unwanted nicknames and doesn't remind you of a former student you had problems with.

Randy was named after a student Roger had who was a nice kid with athletic talent.

Rog was a proud dad and soon became comfortable holding Randy, after he got over his fear of breaking him.

The summer before Randy was born we had opened The Fabric House in a small building uptown, so after the birth, when I taught evening sewing, Roger stayed home with Randy. All seemed to be going well, and he got so he could change diapers without them falling off. This was in the days of cloth diapers, plastic pants and diaper pins, so it was trickier than it is now.

After some time I began to think that my supply of diapers seemed to be smaller than the three dozen I'd received for a shower gift. Upon investigating, I found that anytime Roger had to change a dirty diaper, he simply threw the offensive thing away instead of rinsing it and putting it in the diaper pail.

Sometimes, I assume when he was in a hurry, the diapers that were merely wet would get kicked under the double bed where we laid Randy to change him.

Gross.

Roger and Randy became great buddies. Roger began early coaching him in sports. By the time Randy was six months old, Rog had him sitting up in the hallway and playing catch. The hallway worked great because that eliminated chasing a poorly-thrown ball.

Later when Randy started talking, instead of Mama or Dada, his first word was "ball," much to his dad's delight.

~ ~ ~

The spring after Randy was born, Roger decided he needed to supplement his teaching salary. Many teachers did house painting in the summer, but Rog saw an ad in the local *Jefferson Bee and Herald* newspaper for someone to help at the Dairy Queen. It sounded fun, so he applied and was hired on the spot by the older couple who owned it.

The gentleman was in poor health, so Roger soon learned not only to wait on customers, but how to clean the machines and all the ins and outs of the business. They trained him well, and by early June of that summer, he bought the Dairy Queen for me for my birthday.

Business number two.

We lucked out that summer, as my younger sister, Jeannie, came to stay with us. She worked as an aide at the hospital and helped in The Fabric House by day. In the evenings she took care of Randy while we worked at the Dairy Queen. Even though she needed to get up early to work at the hospital, she would stay up until after we got home from work because we always brought home mistakes (the dipped cones that fell into the chocolate, the malt that got the wrong flavor).

The couple that sold us the business said to always let the workers eat their mistakes and they would not make them so often. That didn't work for us as we never got tired of eating DQ. The three of us would sit up late watching movies, laughing and eating our Dairy Queen. It was a great summer.

The Dairy Queen was lots of fun but lots of work for Roger. Every morning he would go out and clean the machine, and even though I'd be the one to open it when he was still in school he would be the last one to leave it each night because we ran it ourselves, only hiring one person a season. This did cramp our social life, but we would celebrate birthdays and anniversaries by going out to eat after we closed at 11 p.m.

Roger was limited as to how long he could be out of town. One year he went to St. Louis to watch an evening baseball game with the guys and drove home afterward to clean the ice cream machine so I could open up shortly after.

One of the best things about this business was that we could treat others to our product.

Rog's track team would come out at the end of their season and his football team usually got in on malts before we closed for the season. My family loved getting the first quart of the day that we had to weigh to make sure the machine was adjusted correctly.

Our friend, Ray Dillard, has a May birthday, and the only time we had to celebrate was over the noon hour when Roger came out to start the ice cream machine for me.

Since teachers then had an ample amount of time to eat, I would take lunch out and we would celebrate then. One year I made fried chicken and potato salad and ordered a birthday cake.

When I stopped at Saba's Bakery to pick up the cake, I pointed to one in the display case that was decorated with the words "Happy Birthday, Ray."

I said, "I see my cake."

The gal working behind the counter told me that they already had mine boxed up since they knew I'd be in a hurry, so I paid for it and was off and wondering who else named Ray had a birthday that day.

After eating the meal, we opened the box to find a beautifully decorated cake that said "Happy Mother's Day."

We all had a good laugh but didn't have time to go back and get the correct cake, so we ate it. After all, I'd told them which one I thought was mine. We've always wondered what mother got a "Happy Birthday, Ray" cake.

Of course Rog thought that was too good a joke to let die, so many times we've given Ray Mother's Day cards and cakes.

~ ~ ~

Roger was busy year round, with the Dairy Queen open from May through September and teaching and coaching three sports seasons. After a couple years of this routine, someone else opened a fabric shop, so we decided to end that venture in favor of having another child.

Robin joined the family on January 11, 1973. We went to the hospital about three in the morning for her arrival, expecting it would be a fast event.

Roger never liked to miss a day of school so was pleased because he thought he'd be in his classroom in plenty of time that morning. At about 6 a.m. he decided he should call for a substitute, but said he'd be there by noon. Shortly before that, he had to call and say we were still waiting.

Robin was slow to arrive and was a blue baby, having had the umbilical cord wrapped around her neck for some time. She gave us a real scare.

Then after I came home from the hospital everything seemed to go wrong. Robin had to stay in the hospital after I got home, so my mother came early the next morning to take care of Roger, two-year-old Randy and me. Mom arrived right after Roger went to school and as she was walking into the house she noticed her car lights were still on and scurried back to turn them off.

She fell on the ice and broke her wrist. She didn't want to go to the hospital in Jefferson, so I called my dad to come from Dallas Center to get her. My sister, Jeannie, was rousted out of bed by the call and went outside to get Dad. He told her to hop in the pickup and come along with him.

Upon their arrival they found Mom crying from pain, I was crying because she was hurt and leaving, and Randy was crying because we were.

Dad surprised us all by insisting that Jeannie stay and take care of the family.

Imagine Roger's surprise when he came home that afternoon to find my nineteen-year-old sister trying to manage the household. To make matters worse, the sewer backed up as she was doing laundry, all the plumbers in town were busy (we finally called the wife of one and begged for help), the washing machine at the Laundromat wouldn't spin out the water and I cried all the time.

And that was just the first day.

~ ~ ~

Roger spent his time at the hospital with Robin, played with Randy and tried to placate his weeping wife.

With everything going on, we didn't even notice that Jeannie was wearing the same clothes she had arrived in until she mentioned it to me a couple of days later. It was time for a good laugh when she confessed she hadn't known she would be staying and therefore hadn't brought a change of clothes. We quickly rectified that situation. Meanwhile, Robin was getting well enough to come home.

Jeannie added caring for a newborn to her list of duties.

Roger and I had prepared Randy for the addition of a baby to the family, but I guess we hadn't given him all the information he needed. He understood that she would be little, not able to play and would cry when she needed something. What we had neglected to tell him was that she would sleep most of the time.

When we proudly unwrapped our sleeping Robin for him to see, he peered over the blanket at her, looked and started to back up. Of course we were eager for him to fall in love with her, as we had, and asked him why he was backing up.

He answered, "Baby broke. Baby broke."

We assured him that he'd hear her crying plenty before long. I think all three of the adults would admit to being scared to take care of Robin since she'd had a rough start. During the first few days Roger volunteered to take care of Randy while Jeannie and I did most of the baby care.

But it wasn't long before she had her daddy wrapped around her little finger.

~ ~ ~

Jeannie needed to go back to work, so Roger's parents came to visit and get their first look at Robin. Just when all seemed to be going well, I had to go back to the hospital for a few days. Now Roger not only had to visit me, play with Randy, teach and coach, but help more with Robin, as his mother was very nervous about being in charge of a baby girl. After all, her last baby was 33 years old and she'd had all boys.

As I phoned instructions from the hospital, she started feeling more comfortable and got into a routine.

Soon everyone was well and the "Four Rs" were on our own.

Without The Fabric House, I was now a full-time mom and enjoyed playing with the kids at home.

I did surprise Roger one day when he came home from school by announcing that I had a job. The local men's clothing store called and ask if I would be interested in doing alterations for them, and when I said I would be willing to talk about it, the owner said, "I'll be right out."

He brought several pairs of pants to be hemmed, and thus started my in-home sewing business.

Business number three.

But having two kids did not mean that we stayed home all the time, though the years they were small were the years that we were most often grounded. Roger still liked to be on the go, so we were often out and about doing various things. Randy and Robin were the first grandchildren on my side and adored by everyone. That made it all too easy to drop the kids off at my parents when Roger and I wanted to go to Des Moines.

I never knew who enjoyed leaving the kids there more, my parents, Robin and Randy or Rog and I. But now that we are grandparents, I'm guessing it might have been my folks.

SIX

Teaching: Pop or Beer?

Roger began his first teaching job in Jefferson, in eighth grade math. As a new teacher he thought it would be fun to teach in different towns and looked forward to moving to another school district in the future. As time progressed, he realized that teachers often get so caught up with the students and community that they enjoy staying around to watch the kids grow up, and the community and the people in it become your home, so moving just never happened.

Roger retired from the Jefferson district after about 42 years. During that time, he not only taught eighth grade math, but also seventh grade math and finished by teaching sixth grade math. The only moving he did was to change floors from the first floor and end up on the third floor with the sixth grade.

Each grade that he taught was his favorite at the time, but as students became more sophisticated at an earlier age, he found that moving to younger students made them more appreciative of his jokes.

Every student Roger ever had could tell you about the pop bets. He would have cans of pop on his desk and bet with students on college ballgames—he always took the Hawkeyes—and other things. Iowa history is one of his interests, and he would challenge students to try to stump him by coming up with towns he wasn't familiar with.

As students tried the town where Grandma or Cousin Susie lived, his knowledge of Iowa continually added to the pop cans on his desk. But, not wanting to take from the students, he would always try to let them win the sodas back so we always had to buy pop to go with our pizza at home.

It must have been fun to be in Roger's classes, as he was a caring teacher and found lots of ways to make the classes interesting. There were the metric track meets, measuring the room, making presentations about their favorite number and numerous other activities beyond doing worksheets and assignments.

Probably the most well known was the class in which they discussed the number one million and decided they wanted to collect a million of something so they could get a visual image. After much discussion, it was decided to collect something that would also qualify as a community service.

They decided to collect a million pop and beer cans. This project started in the fall, continued all school year and into the summer and the next fall.

Each weekend Roger took his old pickup and would go around to the home of students to pick up the cans they had collected. They could easily collect garbage bags full, as people were still throwing cans in the ditches and around town. The best place to get lots of cans was to check outside the bars on the weekends.

The pile of cans in the field beside our house grew and grew. To keep the students interested, they not only kept count of the growing number of cans, they also had contests. They tried to get cans from far away, unusual cans (my favorite was Old Miss Frothingslosh), different sized cans, series of cans and any other category they could come up with.

Soon his room at school was decorated with the different cans and posters listing the leaders in the different contests. The class not only was the talk of Greene County, they even made the Des Moines Register with an article on the front page of the Iowa section.

In the spring of the year, the mountain of cans was at least 8 feet tall and had a diameter of approximately 20 feet.

One of the neighbors complained that it might attract vermin. The students had reached a half a million cans, had moved on to high school, so decided that would be enough. Now came the problem of what to do with all of them. This was in the days before can deposits, so there was no recycle store to take them. The tin cans were worth next to nothing, as they could only be sold out of state, and the railroad cost would have been as much or more than the redemption money. There was a market for the aluminum cans if they could get them to distributor Farner-Bocken in Carroll. But first the cans had to be separated.

The now-ninth-graders came out on weekends and tossed the mountain of cans into two piles. There was no fast way to do it, as each can had to be checked to see if it was tin or aluminum.

A Jefferson man donated his time and heavy equipment to crush the tin cans, which were then buried.

A local trucker took the aluminum cans to Carroll to be sold by the pound.

After selling the aluminum cans by the pound, the class reaped a respectable amount of money that they needed to decide what to do with. The logical idea was to put it toward their junior-senior prom.

The then-superintendent, Bob Schmidt, thought they should do something special with the money, and it was finally decided that the entire class would go to Kansas City to Worlds of Fun and stay overnight at a nearby Holiday Inn. The school provided five buses to carry the students and chaperones. At that time, coaches drove the buses to games, so several coaches were enlisted to drive the buses and chaperone.

What a great time we all had!

Who would have thought a class discussion about numbers would lead to a unique project that lasted more than a year, cleaned up Greene County, and ended with a huge, fun-filled weekend in another state?

Mr. O and the class also wrote a letter to the state legislature suggesting a can deposit law. Since such a law was presented and passed not too long afterward, they feel they made a difference and were ahead of the times.

Roger had enjoyed this activity tremendously, and at their class reunion in 2010 he was able to display some of the posters and pictures from that year for his former students. Not only that, but this non-drinker still has many of the unusual beer cans that were collected that year and for many years we had a large number of them displayed in our home.

~ ~ ~

Roger is passionate about several things. Probably most of his former students could tell you that he graduated from Hartley High School. Hartley, the town with a heart. I'm sure his students heard that over and over.

He's also a dedicated Hawkeye fan and gets very involved in all of the University of Iowa sporting events. Former students may remember that Roger declared a day of mourning when long-ago coach Ralph Miller announced he was leaving the Hawkeye program.

A school district could not ask for a teacher who was more dedicated to the job. Roger didn't believe in using personal days and was never sick. However, one day I did get him to leave school to come home and rescue me. Randy and Robin were in school and I was a stay-at-home mom on the day I saw a mouse peek out from under the stove. Being terrified of mice, I quickly got up on the kitchen table, reached for the phone on the counter and called the middle school.

I told the secretary I needed to talk to Roger right away. When he got on the line I begged him to come home and get the mouse.

Trying to calm me, he said he'd come home during his free period, but since school was about to start, he couldn't come until about 10 a.m. I finally convinced him to get someone to cover his homeroom while he came home.

Upon his speedy arrival, he brought in our cat and sat her down in front of the stove. Then next time the mouse peeked out, the cat pounced on it and carried it out of the house as Roger opened the front door.

Hurrying back to school, Roger got there for his first class.

My hero!

SEVEN

Coaching

One of Roger's real loves is coaching. When we were first married he was coaching seventh grade football and had never lost a game in the six years he'd been a coach. I do remember how devastated he was with his first loss. I soon learned that it was best to be silent after a loss as he wouldn't be speaking anytime soon, and my chatter would just upset him more.

Being a very caring coach and wanting his team to have every possible advantage, Roger heard about a snack that would be nutritious and provide quick energy, and he decided to give it a try. He was really exited about this snack for his football team. However, he hadn't thought ahead as to how messy and sticky it would be to try to eat honey on oranges right before the game.

Needless to say, he didn't try that snack again.

Former student Leo Brooker has long said his favorite story about Roger took place when he was a running back on Roger's seventh-grade.

The team traveled to Harlan to play a game on a Saturday morning. Upon arrival, Leo discovered he'd forgotten to bring his football shoes.

Roger was not amused. Leo's mother was sent uptown to buy another pair because not having them was inexcusable. Leo had to start the game playing only in his stocking feet. This wasn't as dangerous as it would be today since at that time the young football players wore tennis shoes instead of cleats. However, I doubt that Leo or any of his teammates ever forgot any of their game day gear after that.

This happened in 1968. At that time schools still had money for discretionary spending. On the hour-and-a-half drive home from Harlan, the coaches could buy lunch for the football players. Since there were 40 players from both the seventh and eighth grade teams, it was a sizable order.

The coaches decided on a hamburger and malt for each player. They drove their buses to Cronk's in Denison, where Roger was to place the order for eighty hamburgers and eighty malts. The football players were excited about this meal. However, when the malts came they were all vanilla.

Roger thought that everyone would like vanilla, Roger's favorite flavor.

~ ~ ~

In the early '70s, Jefferson didn't have a girls' basketball team. One of the coaches, Dale Allensworth, got permission to start this sport and coached the girls in junior high. When their grade went to high school, Dale became a high school social studies teacher so he could continue to coach the girls.

To keep the program going, they now needed a middle school coach and asked Roger. He gave up his boys' team and started coaching girls' basketball. He loved coaching the girls, but never quite understood them and had no idea why they could be very emotional and cry for no seeming reason.

For years there were no state guidelines that prohibited coaches having practices with their teams during Christmas vacation. Then came the energy crisis of the late '70s. During the 1979 basketball season, there was a mandate from the state athletic union that teams couldn't practice until December 31. It happened that Roger had a very enthusiastic and talented group of eighth-grade girls who really wanted to play basketball, and they were disappointed about having so many days with no practice.

Somehow, they talked Roger in to having a practice on December 30, at one minute after midnight. Knowing that no parents would be crazy about taking their child to a practice at that time of the night, it was decided it would be fun to spend the night in the gym.

I couldn't believe it when he came home and presented this plan to me. Of course our kids and I were invited, as he needed me to chaperone. Randy and Robin knew several of the players very well, and at age six and nine were excited about the prospect of a slumber party in the gym.

The administration gave permission for this "practice," so it was a done deal.

That semester I was teaching in Scranton. The day before we were to get out for vacation I was driving to work, hit an ice patch on the road, slid and hit a bridge. With 50 stitches in my face and head and many very sore places on my body, I was still to help chaperone the gym overnight.

It was an exciting evening. Roger had lots of games planned for before midnight, including a heavy ball, five feet in diameter, which was rolled back and forth. But the main unplanned activity was running from one doorway to the next to see whose boyfriend was outside. This provided lots of exercise for them and plenty of noise as they hollered back and forth.

At one minute after midnight the practice began. Sleeping came late and was short, but the girls had a great time and I'm sure it's something they've never forgotten. Future classes wanted to have a slumber party in the gym also, but that was a one-time event.

Girls' basketball is a love of Roger's. I don't remember his commenting on the boys' basketball team he played on, probably because that was in the time of the Northwest Iowa powerhouse girls' teams. He still talks about the rivalry between the Hartley Hawkettes and the Everly Cattlefeeders.

A favorite memory of the girls' state basketball tournament was the night a snow storm stranded all the players and fans in Vets Auditorium. A disc jockey was brought in and Rog was among those who danced all night.

Roger coached some really good girls' teams, two of which made it to the state tournament when they reached high school. For years we had season tickets to the girls' state basketball tournament, and one of his dreams was that when we retired we could spend that week in Des Moines and go to all the games. However, six-on-six was what he enjoyed the most and when the state changed to five-on-five games it was never the same to him.

That change came about while Robin was in school, and Roger and one of his former players wore black armbands to school the day the schools officially went to the five-on-five game.

~ ~ ~

Roger began his track coaching with eighth-grade boys. Recently a former track star told us that one of his favorite stories is how he and three other eighth graders were on Roger's 4 x 100 relay team. The middle school Ram Relays had close competition, and Coach Olhausen calculated that the meet winner might be decided during that 4 x 100 relay race.

All four of the students were really good kids who always did their best. To encourage them to work to their maximum ability, he told them that if they won that event, it would not only cinch the win but he would take them to see the Minnesota Twins play.

They won. And true to his word, he took all four of them, in our convertible, to Minneapolis to see a Twins' game that summer.

That former track star said that was the first professional baseball game he'd ever seen, and now he is a huge baseball fan and has attended many professional games.

The year after Jefferson started girls' basketball, the school district committed to starting a girls' track program. He really enjoyed coaching boys' track but believed that girls should have all the chances the guys had, so again it was Roger and Dale Allensworth who became the girls' coaches.

Seven years ago when we retired, he was not ready to get out of coaching and continues to coach girls' track. I'm sure that a bonus to him is that he gets to coach with Teresa Green, the high school business teacher that he's coached with for years. Not only do they have fun coaching together, but she does all the computer work for him. He'd never be able to get his team signed up online if not for her.

Not only does he enjoy coaching, but he has a real talent for it that he has passed down to Robin.

While most coaches valued the use of the computer for making handbooks and figuring stats, again, Roger didn't see the need, so always typed or hand wrote all his handouts to his teams.

His handwriting is legendary. Hardly anyone can read it and even he has trouble reading his notes after they get cold. But I'm sure students still remember some of the notes of encouragement, advice and sports information that covered his blackboard.

For years during the football seasons, he handwrote a weekly football contest for the middle school teachers. I think the teachers had as much fun trying to read his "U Choose Um" contest as they did winning the few dollars in the pot.

As assistant coaches were added in the middle school, Roger had a former college player as his football assistant. They got along great and Terry was a real help.

Being younger, he had up-to-date computer skills and enjoyed doing stats and would email them to Roger. He didn't think too much about not getting a reply since they talked daily at practice. That is, until he got an email back the next August from Roger. It seems that he didn't ever check his email until the school secretary would tell him it was full and he needed to delete some messages. Then, after asking Pat Richards, the teacher across the hall, to remind him how to do it, he would read all the emails as he was deleting and replied to a few. This always took several hours, so it's no wonder he thinks email takes up too much time.

Whatever the sport, Roger concentrated on it and on helping the young athletes do their best. So the day he and another junior high track coach were working changing spikes on track shoes, I'm sure they were talking track and that's why he didn't hear Randy talking.

As he often did, Rog took Randy along with him up to school while he worked. The kids could always find something to do. That particular day they and the other track coach were in the coaches' room working and talking when Randy wanted his dad's attention.

In total concentration, Roger tuned out the sounds of "Dad, Dad" so completely that after a couple minutes, the other coach started saying "Dad, Dad" along with Randy until Roger caught on and finally heard and answered.

ROSEMARIE OLHAUSEN

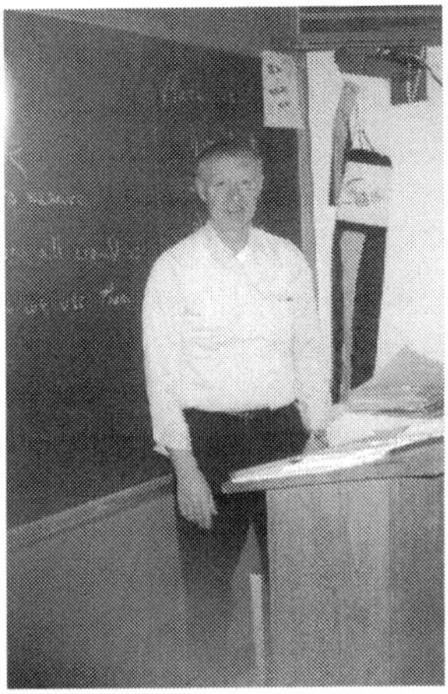

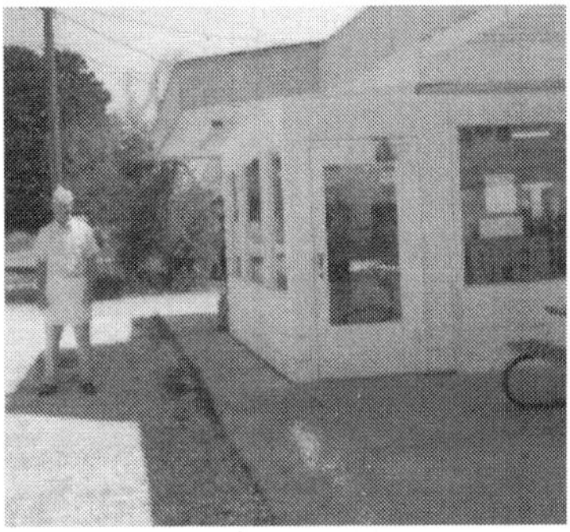

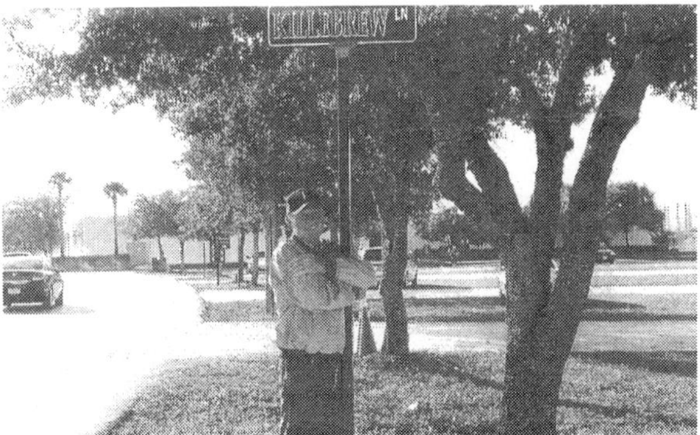
KILLEBREW LN

ROSEMARIE OLHAUSEN

Beta Tau Delta sorority is proud to announce the 2004 Children's Champion award has been presented to Roger Olhausen. Olhausen is a long time resident of Jefferson. He and his wife Rose have taught in the Jefferson and Jefferson-Scranton school district for many years.

Olhausen was chosen as the recipient of the award for his unending dedication to the Jefferson Little League program and the youth of the school district. He began coaching in the early 80s when his son Randy began playing minor league. Soon he joined the Little League board and became the treasurer, a job he held for many years. Olhausen also served as president and secretary of the board. Several seasons he coached two teams, the boys team Randy played for and the girls team his daughter Robin played on. He was always their coach. When Robin moved on to high school in 1987, he remained active on the board until 2002, when he achieved his goal of lighting the girls' field. He always felt their facility should be equal to that of the boys. He also umpired for many years.

Persons who attend any middle school function, athletic or otherwise, will see Olhausen there. He loves to support the students and let them know that he cares. He teaches math in the middle school and coaches football, girls basketball and track.

Olhausen is also very active in the First Presbyterian Church. He has been a Sunday school teacher for over 35 years and also serves as the Sunday school superintendent. He is a member of the Christian education committee.

Roger Olhausen

In the fall of 2002, he retired from the Little League board and now devotes more time to his grandchildren. Their daughter Robin Brand and husband Steve live in Guthrie Center where she coaches girls' basketball. They are the parents of triplets. Randy lives in Jacksonville, FL, where his son Trent is starting to play baseball. The tradition continues. "Thank you, Roger, for all the hours and skill you have given to the youth of our community," a spokespersons said.

Olhausen will be publicly honored at a date in the near future. Anyone wishing to send a card to congratulate him or remind him of special memories may do so at: Box 207, Jefferson, Iowa 50129. Cards should be received by April 30 so he can be presented with them.

MY LIFE WITH ROGER

ROSEMARIE OLHAUSEN

EIGHT

Farmer Roger

Growing up on the family farm in Hartley, Iowa, all the Olhausen boys worked milking the cows. The farm was a mile south of town and across the road from the small airport. Their dad, Edward, sold milk to the school for their lunch program. Every day the boys and Edward would go into town before school and deliver milk. Today's sanitation processes for milk are a far cry from the way things were then. Roger says that they would milk the cows, strain the milk, load it up and take it to town. Of course if a cow stepped in the bucket, they strained the milk twice.

In those days before milking machines, Edward always had cows to milk and they had to be milked twice a day. The boys understood that their help was needed even when it interfered with extra curricular activities at school. If practice was running too late, Roger might have to leave early to go home for milking.

One time a disgruntled coach talked to Edward because his player had to leave to go milk, and in an accusatory voice asked who did the work on the farm. Roger's dad replied, "All of us," and that pretty well settled the disagreement.

Since Roger was the youngest, when he went to college that left his dad to do all the milking. Not surprisingly, when he came home the first time, all the dairy cattle had been sold.

In addition to using the dairy cows for another source of income, they seemed to serve an additional purpose. Roger says he never had a curfew, but it was understood that he had to be ready to milk cows early in the morning. He admits to once coming home from a date during which they had gone to the lakes for the evening and getting home in time to change and do the milking chores.

It seems his car got stuck, or something.

~ ~ ~

Living close to town also meant that they lived close to Harvey Patten, the local truck farmer. During the summer Harvey would drive to Muscatine and get melons that he sold on the square on Saturday nights. All the teens knew Harvey would go to get melons, but no one knew where he kept them hidden. Roger and his friends would often spend Friday nights driving around to find those melons so they could try them out, all to no avail.

Evidently the Olhausen boys were good at keeping secrets, as their dad Edward always let Harvey park his truck in their barn. Their friends never found where the melons were hidden.

Stealing watermelons was a summer evening pastime that Roger's friends still talk about. Thinking they were real sneaky, one night they were raiding the watermelon patch of a girlfriend's family when they were caught. The father snuck up on them, told them he didn't want to see them stealing his watermelons again. And then invited them inside to eat some.

Besides dairy cows, corn and beans, the Olhausens had sheep. . . by the hundreds.

After we had been married a couple of years, Roger and I bought a home on the west edge of Jefferson with more than ten acres of land. Roger thought he was a farmer. The people before us had raised and kenneled dogs, so we acquired a small building with the property, and he decided we could have sheep.

For more than 30 years we always kept a few sheep in the back yard. Not a large number, usually just three or four, but Rog loved having them. He joined the Greene County Lamb Producers and was on the board for a few years. I was always a little embarrassed to go to one of their events and know that we had more toy stuffed sheep in the house than we were raising outside.

When Roger bought his lambs from local farmers, he must have always gotten the talented ones. It never failed that we got sheep that could jump the fences. And they were some of the smarter ones, too. They always jumped over the fence when Roger was gone.

One time they got across the creek and up on the neighbor's hill to the north before someone called to tell me they were out. Roger was teaching and I was home with two little kids. When he got home I was relating to him how I had carried Robin and dragged Randy along as the neighbor and I tried to herd the sheep back home.

After that, many friends and neighbors volunteered or were enlisted to help round up our sheep when they left to find out if the grass really *is* greener on the other side of the fence.

At the beginning of our sheep escapades Roger had his old pickup painted red, white and blue for the 1976 centennial. It wasn't pretty, but he used it to drive to market with his sheep hog-tied. Or sometimes he would have me drive while and he was in the back, trying to hold them down by sitting on them if he hadn't been able to get them tied up sufficiently.

I always appreciated the farmers who would loan him a pickup with high sides on the bed so he could haul the sheep safely, or would actually drive them to the sale barn for him.

A favorite story among our friends is the time Roger took a couple of sheep to Perry to sell at the sale barn on a fall Saturday morning. By then the red, white and blue truck was a thing of the past and he didn't want to bother anyone else to take them, so he came up with an unusual method of hauling sheep.

Fortunately we only had two sheep that year, as he decided that the small station wagon we owned would work fine. As usual, I refused to be a part of this wild idea and was upset that he would use our only mode of transportation for hauling livestock. As he laid down the back seat and covered the floor he assured me that it would be fine. I had no idea how this would work. But Roger enlisted the help of a neighbor, tied up the sheep, and put them in the largest cardboard boxes he could find that would fit in the back of the station wagon, and off he went.

I was still steamed when he arrived home, but the car survived and didn't have any tell-tale signs of the event. However, the story he had to tell will live on forever in our memories.

The trip to Perry had gone as well as could be expected with sheep in the back of the car. Upon his arrival in town he headed toward the sale barn, intent on getting there before the auction started. Roger was driving along and noticed lots of people around but didn't think too much about it at first.

My absent-minded professor had driven into a parade.

Not being able to get to where he was going, he turned off on a side street and got out of the car to watch. Then the sheep started baa-ing. The parade attendees were soon looking around and asking each other if they heard sheep, and where that sound could possibly be coming from. Not wanting to admit that they were in the back of his car, Rog looked around too and admitted that he also heard them. No one found the source of the sound, the parade ended and Roger went on to sell the sheep.

Since we live on an acreage, we have the land beside our home planted by a local farmer in various crops. Roger enjoys going out to visit with him about farming. He especially enjoyed when we had a hay crop. He used to jump up on the hayrack and stack bales like he did in Hartley many years ago. Now giant round bales have replaced the small rectangular ones, so he can't do that any more.

If you grew up on a farm, you know that the bailer doesn't feed in all the hay and there is some left in the field. Knowing that the sheep would love the hay, Roger would take his pitchfork out and pile up what was left in the field. When we didn't have a truck he would have to carry it back to the sheep one pitchfork at a time. The rest of the time, I got enlisted to drive the pickup around the field while he pitched hay in the back. Having also grown up in a frugal farm family, I enjoyed helping on our "farm," as long as I didn't have to do any sheep chores.

~ ~ ~

After selling the Dairy Queen, Roger wanted to make a little money in the summer but still not be tied down to a nine-to-five job. He enjoys being outside and started working for several farmers each summer, walking soybeans to get the weeds out. This can be a daunting job alone, so it became a family thing. We all went out and walked beans for a number of years.

Having grown up on farms we had both done this. I did appreciate that we were making more money than when my dad had paid my siblings and me by the weed. Back then, I remember walking down the rows with my siblings and keeping track of our earnings by loudly proclaiming "eighty-seven button weeds, eighty-eight, eighty-nine" and so on. Times had changed and the farmers now paid more, but I mentioned to Roger one day that none of my friends had to walk beans. He said I should start hanging out with different people.

As the years went by, the bean walking crew changed. First some of Randy's friends joined us to make money. Then a few of Robin's friends walked with us. As our kids got older, they gave it up to do their own thing, and eventually Roger was walking by himself. He never seemed to mind and just enjoyed being outside and doing it on his own time.

That was the case in 1995, when we had friends from the state of Nevada staying with us. As they were ready to go visit relatives for the day, they asked about Roger's whereabouts. Not thinking about the difference in backgrounds, I just answered that he was out walking beans. When the relatives, who are dear friends of ours, asked what Roger and I were doing that day, our guests replied that he was out walking the dog. Puzzled, the friends in town replied that we didn't have a dog.

"Well," the guest said, "Rose said he was out walking Beans."

An explanation about farming followed. That has been a favorite story for years. But, what made it even funnier is that eventually they got a dog in Nevada that they named Beans.

~ ~ ~

Another summer job this math teacher had was driving a bus for crews that went to cornfields to pull the tassels off the corn. Roger would be hired by a seed corn company to pick up the detasselers early in the morning, drive them to the field, and sit and wait for them to either finish or move to another field. He got a lot of books read those summers.

Often, after our kids were up and ready for the day, I would drive them out to the field to spend part of the day with their dad. We'd pack lunches for them, and they had fun playing catch out on the gravel roads and just being with their dad.

As Randy and Robin got older, to make more money, Roger would contract to detassel the corn. As the shortest one in the family, one summer of that was enough for me. I decided there were lots of easier ways to make money, so I retired.

Robin's love of swimming won out, and she started life-guarding, so Roger and Randy were alone in their efforts. They were both tall and didn't feel the work was too hard and the money was good. But I think the summer it was so wet and they had to go out at dawn, in the rain, mud and lighting, wearing heavy trash bags to try to keep some part of their body dry, did give them reason to rethink this choice of income.

Soon, detasseling became a thing of the past for the Olhausens.

~ ~ ~

To stay connected with the farm, Roger has brought home tools, singleton plows, garden gates, a chicken coop—and the list goes on—from his home farm in Hartley. Some of the things he just stores so he knows he has them, other items are displayed outside in our yard. But I thought he went over the top the day we were visiting a small country greenhouse and he saw an outhouse and offered to purchase it. Imagine my shock when the owner told us he could just have it, that it was collapsible and they would take it apart and we could pick it up later in the day.

It is now in the process of being painted, then set up and decorated with a barn quilt and flowers.

Now that we have built a new home farther back off the road on what used to be the sheep pen, Roger's farming has pretty much been eliminated. Or so I thought. Last year he bought two ducks for the grandkids to enjoy. Of course they were thrilled, as anything Grandpa O does is the best. Fortunately for our relationship, he had checked with a farmer before buying them, so after a month or so the ducks would be enjoying a larger farm. Rog and the grandkids loved feeding the ducks and watching them grow.

Roger's not known for his carpenter skills, but he and the grandkids have been working back in our field making a clubhouse. They have all been excited about it and since it's back in an area that is rather out of sight because of some trees, it didn't really matter how it looked as long as they were all having fun. I thought nothing of it the day he was hurrying the kids to get breakfast eaten so they could go uptown with him. They had been gone rather a long time when Summer came running in to get Kaleb, who hadn't gone along, to come see the sheep Grandpa got.

I was more than a little surprised, and went out to find two sheep inside a cardboard refrigerator box in the bed of Roger's pickup. The kids had ridden home in the back and kept the sheep in the box while Grandpa drove. They were *sooo* excited and impressed with how Grandpa could grab the lambs by two legs, lift them out of the box and put them into the pen.

Now, just like before in the original sheep building, the grandkids can go with Grandpa to help feed the sheep. Kameron, at five years old, had missed out on this experience and was excited about the sheep, until she wanted to go in the club house. Now that the sheep have taken up residence there she has pronounced it "Gross."

NINE

The Growing Years

What fun we had while the kids were growing up. Although Roger had said he preferred children to come into our lives when they were already potty trained and ready to play, he ended up loving to play with Randy and Robin when they were still little. He would make all kinds of silly faces and act funny to entertain them. Hide-and-seek was a favorite, with him peeking from behind furniture and around corners, then trying to catch them as they ran away laughing.

Growing up on the farm in Hartley, the Olhausens usually stuck to the basic foods, so Roger is a real meat and potatoes man. His mother always had a big garden and they ate from that as well, but in those days there weren't as many varieties of foods common in most gardens. When we married, Roger believed that the only vegetables worth eating were corn, peas and beans, so he balked when I fixed broccoli, cauliflower, asparagus or any different veggie, and complained that I was trying to feed him grass.

I let this slide until Randy and Robin were old enough to start being influenced by his choices. Then when he would start to say, "You're feeding me grass again," I would give him a kick under the table so he would finish the sentence differently.

It must have worked, because when Robin was planning her eighth birthday party with friends, she requested liver and broccoli for the meal. I diplomatically told her that a special meal like that should be just for the four of us and she could select another favorite to serve her friends.

~ ~ ~

Before we sold the Dairy Queen, when Randy was eight, we all spent a large amount of time there. While Rog and I worked cleaning or making Dilly Bars, the kids played in the back room, often "washing dishes" in the long sink. They loved getting to go across the street and get lunch for all of us from the A & W Drive-In.

Since the DQ occupied most of our summer time, we had to work at finding family time away from the business. One day each summer we would close the DQ and go on a short mini-vacation, usually just to Lake Okoboji in northwest Iowa. Rog would get up early to get the ice cream machine cleaned, and we would head off for the day and overnight so we could get back the day after in time to open up for business as usual.

It was on one of these adventures that we found "the chair."

Taking a break from the pool, we decided to check out the shops in Spirit Lake. While I was browsing in one store, Roger and the kids went ahead to another. Soon Robin and Randy came back, wanting me to move faster and come to the next store because "There is furniture that looks like animals."

Indeed, there were some unique pieces there. The furniture was made from redwood roots and had sheepskins to sit on. Very different. Roger and the kids loved it, and before I knew it he decided to purchase a large footstool that looked like a ram, our hometown school mascot. Knowing that it wouldn't match any of our furniture, he also purchased a large chair to go with it.

Next, came the problem of how to get the furniture home. Both were of solid wood and very heavy. We had just our car and no time for a return trip, so it was decided we would rent a U-Haul.

Arriving home, we were presented with the problem of how to unload this heavy furniture and get it into the house. The solution required four men.

Not our usual souvenir trinket from vacation. Something this unique has been a conversation piece for years, and all company loved trying it out. The chair is fun to sit in but hard to get out of. Randy and Robin were the first in a long line of kids to straddle the ram, hang onto the horns and try to ride this footstool.

~ ~ ~

As Randy and Robin got older, sports became the activity they shared the most with their dad.

Roger put a pitching rubber in our front yard where the kids learned to pitch to him. When they got a little older, there was a basketball hoop outside the garage and a larger court toward the backyard. The field on the south side of the house changed from the community gardens rented out by a local bank to a ball field with backstop, home plate and bases. Farther out in the field, Roger and Randy put up goal posts so Randy could practice kicking with his parents' hopes of a football scholarship.

But although he had fun practicing his kicking, from the time he started Little League, baseball was Randy's sport of choice, with basketball and golf also favored above football.

From the time they were born, Roger indoctrinated our kids in University of Iowa sports. They watched Hawkeye games on television and wore Hawkeye clothes and eventually got to go to Hawkeye football games.

A high point was the vacation the family took to California to watch the Hawks play in the Freedom Bowl in 1984. We flew out, rented a car, did the usual tourist things—Disneyland, San Diego, Crystal Cathedral and Hollywood. But the bowl game was the main event and we were all so excited for our Hawks.

The morning of the game was dreary, and as the game got under way, so did the rain. Roger and the kids were game, and sat down close to the field and cheered the entire time while I sat up under cover. It was a great time. The Hawks won easily.

After the game came the problem. In our excitement to get to the game, we had parked the rental car, jumped out and ran to the stadium. Now we had no idea where the car was. Since this was before remote buttons, we couldn't make the car honk, lights flash or trunk lid go up. We had to just wait under the overhang until the parking lot was almost empty before we spotted a lonely little blue car. Roger ran out, tried the key and when it opened the car, we all piled in and off we drove.

Since then, we've made more of an effort to remember what we rented.

Randy and Robin are the oldest of the cousins on my side of the family, so we were all excited when younger cousins came to visit. The nieces and nephews remember how much fun Uncle Roger was. His favorite activity after each meal was to wad up his napkin and throw it at them, which started everyone throwing theirs at each other. I think some of them got in trouble when they went home and tried doing that.

Emily, our youngest niece, remembers being profoundly embarrassed when Roger hung her swimming suit on the antenna on top of the house.

Roger played ball with them and taught some of them how to throw, catch and pitch. When we had family dinners, Roger was the one who organized the ballgames in the afternoons. The trunk of our car always contained sports gear, so in the fall there was flag football and during spring and summer we were loaded with bats, balls and gloves for softball games.

People driving by have often commented on seeing everyone outside playing ball and how they thought we must be having lots of fun.

And they were right.

Now that all nieces and nephews are adults, they still enjoy Roger's fun-loving and funny ways. When he was teaching, he bought them Christmas presents he selected from the prizes given out for middle school magazine sales. As they got older, they appreciated the thought and could use things like the calculators, but really enjoyed the novelty, silly things such as the screeching monkeys that fly across the room, lighted bouncy balls and finger lights. One of the adult nephews wore the lighted sunglasses to a night-time sand volleyball game and impressed all his teammates.

As a boy, Roger did some hunting but hadn't for many years. When he heard the nephews planning a deer hunt, he asked to join the group and of course, they were glad to have him.

The Saturday of the deer hunt they all collected at the farm and were planning who would hunt where. Since Roger didn't want to hunt, preferring just to walk along, he was to stay along a fence line so everyone knew where he was and he would be okay.

All the guys returned to the house at noon, but Roger was missing. No one had seen him. When he didn't show up later, the nephews got worried and went looking. One of them finally found him, walking around just enjoying the scenery. He said he wasn't lost, just wasn't sure where he was or how to get back to the farmstead.

TEN

Mr. Little League

Our time with the Dairy Queen was great, but as Randy approached the age for Little League, sports won out over a summer job. We sold the DQ so we could spend a large part of our summers at the ball fields.

Roger started coaching Randy's minor league baseball team and continued to coach his teams until high school, where there were paid coaches.

When Robin started minor league softball, Roger had me sign up as the coach. Of course, I was the coach in name only while he did most of the work. He also coached Robin's teams until she could play high school softball.

When Roger gets involved in an organization, he really commits himself. Before long he was not only doing volunteer coaching of both Randy's and Robin's teams, he was on the Little League board and had me helping in the concession stand and keeping the team scorebook. Besides the time spent at the ball fields for games and practices, he prepared the fields and painted the stands and dugouts.

Athletes don't become good by just going to practices, so he worked with Randy and Robin for hours on end, pitching in the front yard. That didn't end until Randy was throwing so hard that it was dangerous for Roger to be catching him. Of course, if Roger had worn protective equipment, that would have helped prevent many of those bruises he got.

Our family was so into baseball and softball that Roger erected a backstop in the field beside our house and dug in a pitcher's mound and home plate. Many a practice was held on Olhausen field when our children were younger. Now it's in use again for our grandchildren and neighborhood kids.

Roger had grown up playing ball, so it was natural to have softball games on the 4th of July when we journeyed to Hartley for his father's birthday celebration. Each year we loaded up extra balls, gloves and bats in anticipation of the family fun, with all ages joining in the game. The adults on my side of the family didn't really get into this, but Roger always played football or softball with my nieces and nephews at family dinners.

As Randy and Robin outgrew Little League, I thought that Roger would too, but he enjoyed the kids and the sport so much that he stayed active for 24 years. Although he didn't coach all that time, he continued to be on the board as their treasurer, umpired some games, painted, put up signs and was the person everyone turned to when there were questions about how things should be done.

One of the big expenses for Little League was the team uniforms, and Roger, as treasurer, was always in charge of contacting businesses to sponsor the teams and pay for the uniforms. Hopefully these would last several years, so he tried to impress on coaches and parents the importance of making sure the kids weren't wearing them except for games and turning them in at the end of the season. He despaired at the condition of some uniforms when they came back and enlisted my help washing and mending.

Ballplayers who didn't get their uniforms turned in could expect to have him show up at their home to collect them.

Roger finally ended his formal ties with Little League when Robin had her children and he didn't want to miss out on any time with the grandkids. But in the decades that he was associated with the organization, there were few activities he wasn't involved in.

In 1992 the district honored him by naming him the Volunteer of the Year, and in 2003, when he finally gave up all involvement except for being an occasional umpire, the local board presented him with an appreciation plaque. He was recognized in 2005 by Beta Tau Delta for his work with Little League, church and school with the Children's Champion award presented at Bell Tower opening ceremony. He was especially proud to receive this award with his children and grandchildren in attendance.

Now, with grandchildren, Roger has again gotten into the youth sports, coaching them as they learn. When we drive to Florida to visit Randy and Trent, he takes along his baseball glove, bats and balls to practice with Trent whether it is in parking lots or on ball fields.

Back in Iowa, Roger had to learn the basics of soccer so he and Robin could coach the triplet's first ball team. At the age of six they started playing co-ed softball, and once again Robin and Grandpa were the coaches.

~ ~ ~

It's hard to tell who looks forward the most to the games of catch in the yard, Roger or the grandkids. But probably Roger, since as we get older we realize that these times won't come around again and we need to avail ourselves of all the opportunities to play with them. Even now, as we live an hour and a half away, Robin continues to list her dad as assistant coach, and we eagerly drive the distance to help and to cheer them on.

But that's no different than what most grandparents would do.

ELEVEN

Entering the Twenty-First Century

As the year 2009 comes to a close, I'm reminded of the Frank Sinatra song, "It Was a Very Good Year." It has been a very good year, but also a very BIG year for Roger. Not one to jump at new fads or changes, he has resisted becoming thoroughly modern. Originally he had hoped that he would be able to retire before computers became a big part of the education system. He did his best to ignore all the advantages, and Pat Richards always took pity on him and helped put his grades on report cards and any other project that demanded the use of the computer.

Many times I've told our children, "If anything happens to me, you might as well sell the stove, microwave, computer, TV remote, cell phone, DVD and VCR."

Roger thought it was good exercise to get up off the couch and change the TV channels, so I was the only woman I knew who had sole control of the remote. Not really a bad thing.

One of our children's favorite stories was about the time Robin, son-in-law Steve, Roger and I went to Kansas City to meet with Randy. He flew in from Florida for the weekend to watch a Florida State football game, so we went down to spend time with him.

The four of us stayed in a motel, and Randy stayed with a college friend. We all had a good time, and Sunday morning we were to meet with Randy for a late breakfast before taking him to the plane to fly back to Florida. As I was headed to the shower to get ready for the day, I handed Roger the phone number to call and asked him to use my cell phone to get hold of Randy and arrange the time and place to meet.

When I came out of the bathroom, Roger was facing the window of the motel, trying to call. He told me the cell phone wasn't working. About that time the TV came on. He'd been trying to call by using the TV remote and hadn't figured out why he couldn't get through, but the TV kept going on and off!

Randy and Steve about fell off their chairs at breakfast when I told them that one!

~ ~ ~

Before we got married, Roger told me that he wasn't a cook. His German mother was a wonderful cook but didn't teach her boys any domestic skills. To this day, he doesn't do any cooking, not even grilling.

Before we were married, he had decided to fix a frozen pizza one evening. That didn't go well, as he had a gas stove and didn't know how to light it, and got a small explosion instead of supper.

The year I took a sabbatical from school to help Robin and Steve with their newborn triplets, I would often get home from Guthrie Center late in the evening after Robin and Steve returned to their home from coaching the GC girls' basketball team. One night I got home after 10:30 p.m., tired and hungry.

Roger had been keeping the official book for the Jefferson teams so hadn't been home very long when I arrived. He surprised me by asking if I was hungry, and said he was too.

My first thought was that I now had to fix a meal. But he said, "Good. I put a frozen pizza in the oven."

I was thrilled—we had an electric stove—and asked when it would be done. He didn't know, but said it had been in for about 20 minutes.

I was excited that we could have some nourishment soon so said I'd check on it. I tried, but the oven door wouldn't open.

Rog said he didn't want it to fall open (When had *that* ever happened?) so he'd moved the lever on the door to lock it.

That he did! It meant that the oven was locked like it was in the cleaning cycle and would not unlock until the temperature lowered.

I wasn't happy about this and turned the oven off. After hearing me complain and state that now there would be no pizza because the door wouldn't open, he decided to take matters into his own hands. When he started to get out tools, determined to open it, I knew enough to walk into the other room before coming unglued.

He did find out that it was indeed locked and there was nothing he could do to open it. There was another pizza in the freezer that I said could be put in the oven when it finally cooled down enough to open, because I knew this one would be beyond eating.

About a half hour later we tried the door, and the oven had cooled enough that the door opened.

Roger had been saying that he knew we would be able to eat the pizza, but it was *very* browned. He insisted it would be okay if I would just cut it, that we didn't need to eat the crust.

I could see a distinct line all the way around that seemed to be where the cheese met the crust. I always cut pizza with my kitchen shears, so I got them out and attempted to cut into the pizza. Try as I might, I just couldn't get it cut! I finally realized that he hadn't just put the pizza on the pan, he'd left it on the cardboard and that was what I was trying to cut.

Once I got the pizza separated from the cardboard, we did crunch on some of it. Remember, we were both starved. But the worst of it was that now we had to buy a new oven because the door was sprung from when he'd tried to pry it open.

Needless to say, I never ask him to cook anything.

However, one time I did count on him to help around the kitchen. The middle school teachers used to bring food one day a week for the teachers' lounge. One evening about 10:30 p.m., Roger suddenly remembered that the next day was his turn to take treats, so he asked what I could make at the last minute. I suggested he stop uptown on his way to school and purchase a couple dozen donuts since it was nearing bedtime.

He really wanted to take something homemade, so we reached a compromise. He would run to the store and buy brownie mixes which I would mix up and put in the oven before retiring for the night. He would stay up and take them out of the oven when they were done.

It was after eleven when I went to bed, having given instructions to him to take the brownies out when the timer went off.

The next morning when I went to the kitchen to frost the brownies, they were nowhere in sight. After looking all over, I asked Roger what he'd done with them after removing them from the oven. He replied that he hadn't been sure they were done so he'd just turned off the heat and left them in the oven.

As a home-economics teacher, I was appalled and knew they were now hard as a rock. When I told him he would have to buy donuts after all, he still wanted to take the brownies to school. My reputation as a cook was at stake, but he insisted.

So I ended up frosting them and off he went to school with two pans of petrified chocolate.

Later that afternoon in the high school hallways, I was stopped by a faculty member from the middle school who told me he'd gotten a laugh at Roger's note.

It said: "Rose baked these. I was supposed to take them out of the oven. I didn't. She said you'd never eat them. I told her you'd eat anything."

Not only did the teachers eat them, they needed so much muscle trying to cut them they had made holes in my pans.

But back to why this was a very big year for Roger. Our kids are slowly moving him into modern times. First, we needed to get a television for upstairs since we had had a large opening built in the entertainment center for one, and it looked a little bare with that empty hole. Little did he know that new televisions don't have buttons on the front to control them and a remote is necessary to operate the television.

Now, when it is basic channel changing or volume control, he has the remote.

Next came a new cell phone. I've been on Robin and Steve's friends and family plan, and when we all got new phones they got a very basic one for Roger. After several lessons from the grandkids, and a little prompting from me, he can now call and text to family members and hasn't changed the television channels once with his new phone.

But Christmas brought the biggest change when Santa (aka our kids) brought him a laptop computer.

When we'd lived in the other house I'd had my computer in his den. When we moved, one stipulation was that the computer couldn't be in his den, so I'm writing this while sitting on the bed in the guest room.

So far, he's able to turn the laptop on and off and play solitaire. Stay tuned for updates on how that's progressing.

He had been so sure that if he had a laptop of his own, he'd be able to learn how to use it. That remains to be seen, as it's been sitting on his desk doing nothing but collecting dust for the last six months.

Steve commented that it was a rather expensive paper weight.

TWELVE

On the Road Again

Willie Nelson may have sung the song, but we lived it. I have never liked to ride in a car for long periods, so this was another quirk of Roger's that I had to get used to. For years I was treated like a child when I'd ask if we were about there or could we stop for a break. He would just patiently reply that he'd turn off at the next town, but time and time again he would miss the turn.

I was on to his ways but never figured out how to change him. So on we rode.

Roger is a good driver and fearless. Like the slogan the post office used to have that neither hail nor sleet nor snow will prevent the delivery of our mail, no weather prevented us from going places.

This was really brought home to me when Randy was a little over a year old. Roger was a delegate to the teachers' meeting in Des Moines and left early that school morning, dropping Randy off at my parents for a couple of days. I was left in town to substitute in Roger's math class and was to ride down to my parents' after school with another teacher, meet Roger there for supper and stay overnight in Des Moines with him.

The winter day took a turn for the worse and by the time school was dismissed, the teacher I was to ride with had decided not to brave the weather by driving that distance. He offered me a ride home.

Upon arriving, I realized that Roger had taken the house keys and I had no way to get in.

Now what?

I would have to stay with some distant relatives in Jefferson, so was dropped at their door and left to explain my situation. I needed a place to spend the night, needed to call my parents so they and Roger would know why I didn't show up for supper, and I also didn't have any extra clothes since Roger had taken them with him.

They were most gracious, but I was embarrassed. We were having supper when Roger showed up at their door. He had come through the blowing snow with the house keys to take me home.

My hero. If the weather was better the next day, we could go to Des Moines.

I don't think we ever told anyone, but as soon as we left the relatives' home we headed straight to Des Moines. Staying in a motel was a rarity we didn't want to miss so we braved the weather and traveled the nearly seventy miles, barely able to see the edge of the road.

We did discuss the fact that we were not being too responsible since we now had a child to think of, and vowed to be more careful in the future.

When Randy was born, we still had our blue convertible. It scares me now to think of driving with him in just a little plastic carrier that wasn't secured. It was years before seat belts were standard car equipment. I have a vivid memory of slamming on the brakes when someone pulled out in front of me in town. Randy was in the infant seat on the front seat and the seat went sliding to the floor. He was fine, but I was really upset.

Even though Roger is a good driver, he is still a guy and that means he always thinks he knows where he's going and doesn't want to ask directions.

He's known for taking the back roads. We were married for years before I could find my way to Hartley on my own because he tried to take a different route each time we went there.

When Randy and Robin were both middle school age we drove to Kansas City to see a baseball game, and since we weren't in any big hurry, Rog decided to avoid the busy highways and take the back roads to enjoy the scenery. We saw mostly farms and seemed to be getting farther and farther away from the main road. I wasn't too impressed with traveling on gravel roads, but when we got to the one-lane dirt road, that's when Randy, Robin and I insisted we find something not quite so rural.

I enjoy scenery as much as anyone else, and Roger and I like to visit new places. Coming home from a wedding in northeastern Iowa we decided to drive along the Mississippi River. It was lovely, but the highway wasn't always close enough to the river to suit Roger, so when we drove through one town he decided to find the road that would be closer so we could enjoy a better view.

Once again we found ourselves on a gravel road. It's always fun to look at houses and farms and we weren't on any time schedule, so just enjoyed the winding road that seemed to go on and on without intersecting with another one that might take us closer to the river. After about half an hour I mentioned that we seemed to be going to our right more than straight. Fifteen minutes later, I started seeing farmsteads and homes that we'd already gone by, but it took longer for Roger to see anything he recalled from our tour.

We'd gone in a pretty big circle.

We did start to curtail some of the driving in bad weather once we were parents. However, some of Iowa's worst weather can occur on what seemed earlier to be a nice day. That was the case on April 29, many years ago when we went to Hartley on a Sunday morning.

When we left Jefferson after Sunday school, the sun was shining and we didn't see even a hint of bad weather when we arrived at Roger's folks' for Sunday dinner. In the afternoon we drove out to the family farm to see how it had been fixed up. After a leisurely tour we headed back outside to our car, only to find it covered with an inch of heavy slush. When I suggested it might be a good idea to head for home, Roger assured me that this bad weather was about to end and I had nothing to worry about. So we returned to his parents' home for more visiting.

By the time I finally convinced him that it wasn't getting any better, the ground had about six inches of slush. For once, he decided that the weather warranted staying on the main highway, so we headed the eighteen miles toward Spencer. Our vehicle at that time was a small station wagon that sat low to the ground. Soon the bottom of the car was dragging in the slush as Roger tried to drive in the tracks of others. Before we even got to Spencer, we were stuck in the middle of the road.

We sat there for a few minutes, wondering what to do. A man stopped, introduced himself as a minister and offered us a ride to a neighboring house.

We didn't have much choice, so found ourselves getting in his old car that was dirty and had springs sticking through the seat in the back. He must have had a very small and poor congregation.

Randy, Robin and I were left at the house where some of his parishioners lived while Roger rode on to Spencer to find someone to get our car moved. I don't care for animals inside, and there were pets there. The kids and I were in an uncomfortable position of not wanting to offend the people who were giving us shelter from the storm but at the same time not wanting to sit or eat in this house that made me appear to be a Martha Stewart in comparison.

It seemed to take forever before Roger and the tow truck driver came back with our car, but it was probably only a couple hours. When they returned, the four of us all piled into our car, which was being towed backwards.

On the way to Spencer, Roger asked the three of us what it would take to keep us quiet about this latest adventure. Randy asked for a four-wheeler, and Robin was also quick with a request. Roger offered to redo our kitchen if I could forget this had happened. I responded that I knew he didn't have enough money to keep me quiet about this.

After being towed into town, we and the car were dropped at a repair shop. The mechanic on duty said he thought once all the slush thawed off we would be able to drive the car again. He was correct. As we left his shop, he told us that even the tow trucks weren't going out on the roads and recommended motels for the night. Roger was sure the roads would be fine, so off we went.

Now we were headed south, toward Storm Lake. Again, he was trying to keep our car in any tire tracks along the way, which was difficult since our wagon had a narrow wheel base. We slowly drove for miles, occasionally seeing vehicles off the side of the road.

At one gas station there were several cars parked and the drivers waved to us to come in, but Roger kept on going.

We seemed to be driving for a long time without finding a town. Robin had to go to the bathroom, but there were none to be seen, and besides, we knew if we stopped we might not get going again.

All of a sudden we seemed to be in a town. All was dark, but when the lightning flashed (It was green lightning. Really.) we could make out houses.

We had arrived in Storm Lake, but the weather was still ugly. Although Rog was determined to keep going, we were forced to stop at a stoplight that wasn't working because the car in front of us had stopped.

We were stuck again. A policeman came over and told us someone would pull the car around to the fire station across the way and we should stay there for the night. Robin, Randy and I got out and ran to it since it was sure to have a bathroom. Unbelievably, the first person we saw in the fire station was a former student who had been in Jefferson for the weekend and was returning to college in northwest Iowa. He was stuck there too, as were about a dozen other travelers. It so happened that his mother was a school secretary, so when he called her, we explained that we would be late for school the next day and asked her to arrange for our classes to be covered. The weather in Jefferson was fine, so we were glad he could vouch for our story.

As I recall, the firemen made us popcorn and had a small television, but it was a pretty boring evening. We all ended up trying to sleep under tables on the floor of the fire station.

Monday morning we awoke to find the sun shining and the six to eight inches of slush mostly melted. We hopped in the car and headed for Jefferson.

Along the way we discussed the probability that the track meet that day would be cancelled because of all the water from the slush.

Jefferson had not gotten any of this crazy weather, so we all took showers, hurried to school and had a story that sounded so bizarre that people almost doubted it. Since this happened at the end of April, any time before the fourth of July when we go to northwest Iowa I make sure to have my snow boots in the car.

Sometimes it seems as though Roger is trying to see how many miles we can get on the car in a given period of time, but often our plans have changed so fast that the car barely stops as we change direction.

That was the case the summer when Robin was ten and Randy was twelve. Little League had just finished for the season, so we had time to ourselves and decided to drive an hour and a half to Marshalltown to watch the high school baseball team play in the state tournament and then journey on to visit friends in Illinois. We were packed and ready to go when someone stopped and asked if Randy could play on a traveling team that would have their first practice and games three days later on the other side of the state. Everyone was excited, and it was agreed that we could be in LeMars for the practice and games.

Off we went. Our team won and we were delighted that their next game would be on our way home from Illinois so we could watch the Rams again, which we did. And they won a second game. We arrived home late that night, picked up fresh clothes and Randy's baseball equipment and were on the road again.

Now I was getting a little stressed as the next weekend was my parents' fortieth wedding anniversary. I had planned to have plenty of time at home to bind a quilt I'd made for them for the occasion. So said quilt was loaded in the car with us.

Off we went to Randy's game, which they won. After the celebrating, we hopped in the car and headed half way across the state to the next game of the high school baseball tournament. Sadly, they lost that time, but at least that would be our last trip to Marshalltown.

While Roger drove, I sat beside him with the quilt spread out, sewing the binding. I hadn't realized that if Randy's team won, they would be playing on Saturday, the day of the anniversary.

The day of the anniversary party, Robin and I went to the farm and helped set up and get the food ready. Roger and Randy weren't expected until evening. I wasn't pleased that baseball had won out over the momentous occasion, and didn't tell anyone where they were. I fielded questions by reassuring everyone that they would be coming shortly after the party started. When they did arrive, both Randy and Rog were excited because not only had his team won, the next tournament Randy would be playing in was in Wyoming.

On the road again.

~ ~ ~

More than forty years of marriage has brought an interesting assortment of vehicles into our lives. First were the two convertibles. Those were sporty and lots of fun, but driving in all the town parades would probably be the best memories. Many a homecoming queen or attendant sat on the back of those cars as well as our dear friend and neighbor, 1972 Olympic Gold metal archery winner, Doreen Wilber.

The old pickup was added when we owned the Dairy Queen. It was useful since I needed the car while Roger was teaching. This was the one that would later haul pop and beer cans. It was so old that in 1976 for the centennial Roger let the girls who babysat for us paint it red, white and blue.

This distinctive pickup would become part of one of Roger's most interesting adventures. After several years, this pickup had served its purpose for Rog and he was ready to get rid of it. After an ad came out in the local paper, a former student showed up at the door to inquire about purchasing it.

In all the years he taught, Roger always saw the best in each of his pupils, but as an adult, this one wasn't someone he would trust too far. He had really scary eyes and looked mean. However, he wanted to buy the truck, so he and Roger discussed the purchase price and the fact that it would be sold on a red title, which meant that before it could legally be driven, the new owner would need to fix it up and register it at the courthouse.

The purchaser agreed to the price and said he would register the pickup. It was a done deal, and he took off in the truck.

All went well for several weeks until one day Roger was called in to his principal's office and found that he was in trouble with the sheriff. It seemed that the red, white and blue pickup was the get-away vehicle in a robbery—and it was still registered in Roger's name.

He explained the purchase deal but was told that since the registration had not been changed, and although they believed him, he was in a lot of trouble.

Rog consulted an attorney who confirmed he could indeed be charged with this crime unless he could get the alleged robber to go to the courthouse and change the registration.

What to do?

After thinking this over for some time, Roger came up with a plan. He would get the truck back until the registration was changed.

Easier said than done.

Since the person who'd bought the truck lived out in the country, Roger scoped out the house and decided that I would take him out to this place and he would sneak in and get the truck. It didn't sound like a good idea to me, but not wanting him to go by himself, I was drawn into the plan.

Feeling like Bonnie and Clyde, we waited for the cover of darkness before heading out into the country. Luckily, Roger still had a key he'd forgotten to give the purchaser, so after I left him out down the road from the farmhouse, he carefully and quietly crept into the yard, staying out of sight of the house. He got in the truck, quickly started it up and sped off into the night.

We were never so glad to get home.

Now Roger just had to get the new owner to transfer the registration at the courthouse. The man turned up at our home the next day and asked if Roger had his truck. Roger admitted he did and explained that he had gotten it because the registration still needed to be transferred and said if they could go to the courthouse together and do this, he could have the truck back. That was agreed upon and off they went to take care of business.

After the title was transferred, the man rode off in what was now truly his truck, and Roger went to the sheriff's office. After he showed them that the title was transferred, the sheriff wanted to know where the alleged robber was now. Roger replied that that was their job. He'd saved himself, but would let them find the new owner of his truck.

One day Roger came home from Boone with a new car. We hadn't even discussed buying a new car and that he would do this without my knowledge, let alone my consent, really upset me. It was a bone of contention for a long time.

However, we literally didn't use this car for months. It just sat in the garage so it wouldn't get any miles on it. Another small quirk of Roger's that I didn't understand.

Once we finally started to drive it, this car became like part of the family. After it served its time as the family car, then it became the kids' car. It only got sold after it was in a state of disrepair. A car dealer in Des Moines had an advertising campaign that said they would take any car, regardless of its ability to run, as a trade-in. So one fall day, Roger jump-started it (the only way to get it to run) and took off for the dealership.

He knew he couldn't stop along the way as he wouldn't be able to get it going again. After casing the vehicles on display and selecting the one he wanted, he found a salesman and started making a deal for a small pickup on the lot.

The car still looked okay, but when the dealer said he wanted to take it for a spin, Roger walked away. Later, when the salesman found him and said that he'd not been able to start the car, Roger just commented that, "Sometimes it starts a little hard."

The deal was made and we had a nice Ford S10 pickup that would be with us for several years.

~ ~ ~

Another of Roger's adventures on the road occurred the first fall after we retired. He volunteered for us to go out to the Tetons and help our friend Ray Dillard drive back after his summer working at the Grand Teton Lodge.

It sounded like a great adventure. We'd fly out, spend a few days and drive back with Ray. We'd forgotten that Ray's having spent five months required that he had a packed car and there wouldn't be room for two extra passengers.

Plan B was that Rog would go, turn around and come back. After checking on the cost of air travel there he decided to go by bus. However, Greyhound only went as far as Rock Springs, so it was arranged that he would meet Ray there.

Since I'm usually in charge of travel plans, I was worried about sending Roger off, but he was excited. The tickets were ordered. The excitement mounted.

Departure time was 4:30 a.m., so we spent the night in Des Moines and I drove him to the bus depot. That was where reality set in. As he checked on his departure, he noticed that there didn't seem to be anyone going his way that looked like they would become a close friend. A bummer for someone who loves to visit. He walked me back to the car, where I locked myself in and watched him board the bus.

I went back to bed as he started his adventure. Hours later, when I returned home, I waited for his phone call to see how far he'd gotten. We were both disappointed when he called early afternoon and was still sitting three hours away in Omaha. That seemed to be how the day would go, with the bus stopping for change of passengers or drivers and bathroom or food breaks. The chance of him arriving later that evening in Rock Springs looked bleak.

Indeed, there were many stops. They finally arrived at Rawlins, a town about three hours from his destination, at 4 a.m. The bus driver announced that this was the last stop made by Greyhound and that Roger, the last passenger, would be picked up by someone else and taken to Rock Springs. Being dumped out at the edge of an unfamiliar town in the middle of the night was not something he had expected when we purchased the ticket, so he was unsure of what to do. The bus drove off, and he was alone.

While he stood thinking about what to do next, a van pulled up and the driver asked if he was the passenger to Rock Springs. When Roger said he was, the driver told him to climb in, and off they went.

Rog caught a couple hours of sleep and arrived at his destination about 6:30 a.m. This time, he was deposited at a gas station and left wondering how to get to the motel where he and Ray had arranged to meet that evening.

His luck had finally turned around and he found it was just across the street. Ray is a creature of habit and had stayed at this motel many times. When Roger went in and asked if they could keep his small bag until check-in time, they said they had saved Ray's usual room and Roger could check in then and take a nap before looking over the town.

The guys met up later that afternoon and had a good trip home, but I think that cured Rog's desire to ride the bus or go somewhere without me.

THIRTEEN

I Had a Dream

Awake or asleep, Roger is a source of entertainment. However, I'm usually the only one who has heard all about his dreams.

It's been my understanding that most people do not remember their dreams. At least a couple times a month Rog will wake up and have had a dream to tell me about. They usually involve an odd assortment of people that he knows, although some may be from long ago. The situations he gets in during his dreams are uniquely different.

After over forty years of marriage, I was finally in one of his dreams, but recently he dreamed about the grandkids. At the present time they live in Harlan, which is about eighty miles away. In his dream he was supposed to take them to school. Not a hard task usually, but he'd had to walk the eighty miles from Jefferson to Harlan to take them to school.

Recently he had a new setting for a dream. He wanted to be in the circus and had attempted several jobs that didn't work out for some reason. Then he got the idea to work with the animals. The boss man was a little leery. He asked what previous experience Roger had to qualify him to work with lions, tigers and elephants. With great confidence Rog replied that he had worked with sheep and ducks so thought the wild animals wouldn't be any problem.

FOURTEEN

I Might Need That—Boxes and Boxes

Roger is a collector. He has an elephant collection, coin collection, baseball card collection, ice cream dipper collection, beer can collection and probably some others that I've forgotten. While most of us have kept a few mementos from our past, his collections go beyond that. I'd eaten my share of Cracker Jacks, played with the prize and lost or tossed it. Roger still has a number of his prizes as well as autographed pictures and toys advertised on cereal boxes that he had sent away for more than fifty years ago.

As a kid in Hartley, Roger was a sports fan, especially of the Minnesota Twins baseball team. Since we're talking way before television, he used to listen to their games on the radio with his family. He still has the notebooks where he wrote down the players and kept the score as the games went along.

Being a baseball fan, he also collected baseball cards. Roger wasn't a Yankees fan, so he doesn't have any of the famous Yankees baseball players' cards, as he usually traded them for some of his favorites. His best ones are from the early '50s.

I remember well when he first took part of his collection to a baseball card show in Des Moines.

Randy and Robin were elementary age and we were headed somewhere else, but Roger and Randy stopped at the card show while Robin and I went shopping.

At that time he kept his favorite old cards in a red velvet cigar box. He was amazed to have several dealers eyeing the box, following him around and asking to see what he had. As he was later telling me what a couple of them were worth, the kids and I were saying, "Yeah, we can all go out and eat on that card. We could stay at a motel if you sold that card."

The one that was really worth a lot was his Willie Mayes Giants card. Being young parents struggling with finances, I thought selling this card would be a great idea. He has sworn that he'll never sell it because of the special memories.

As a longtime Willie Mayes fan he was excited, when he was in college, to hear that this hero would be coming to play in Des Moines for the Iowa farm team. Roger had to go. When he arrived, the stadium was sold out and he could only get a standing-room ticket. In those days that meant standing around inside the fence, all around the outfield. He ended up standing in center field and says that Willie was only about ten feet from him. It is one of his favorite memories and the reason he is keeping that card.

Roger is still a collector of baseball cards but now has some in plastic sheets in a three ring notebook while others are in various boxes. Through the years he has purchased thousands of cards for himself and Randy, and now he is enjoying teaching his grandsons the fun of collecting baseball cards.

No one, including Roger, knows what is in some of the boxes he has stored.

Before we built our new home he had rented a storage unit in town. I had no idea about this until I unsuspectingly opened a bill for rent on said unit. To this day I have no idea what was in it, but I have a feeling that whatever it was now resides in this house or one of the outlying buildings. When our home was being built, our contractor included an area that could be used as a storm shelter under our front porch. The porch doesn't look too large, but the space under it looked huge, and Roger was thrilled and announced that this area would be for his storage. Then he proclaimed that it would easily hold more than one hundred boxes and that he would be moving them in some day when I was gone.

Well, it happened.

Later he confessed that he brought more than a hundred boxes home when he had retired. When I retired from the high school, I can only recall bringing a half dozen boxes.

What, might you ask, could have been in the boxes he brought home? If he should be called upon to start teaching middle school math in our home, he has plenty of worksheets and textbooks. There are worksheets from all three grade levels of math he taught, and not just one of each one, but sometimes dozens. Occasionally he will run across some from the early years of his teaching career that were made on mimeograph machines. They've lost the smell of that machine but the blue ink is still good. He also has worksheets, tests and notebooks from some of his students.

Roger's favorite math textbook was made by Laidlaw in the '60s. Without asking the teachers, the administrators selected a new math series. As is often the case, the people selecting weren't math teachers and the new series was harder for the students to understand, and not to Rog's liking. Even though the former books looked far from new, he felt they still had worth and kept a large number of them instead of tossing them all in the dumpster.

Imagine the surprise of the former neighbor boy, now a doctor, who came to visit us and went home with his eighth grade math book.

But those aren't the only books in boxes. Roger has many of his college textbooks, as well as the little blue folders used for taking college tests. Other boxes contain books from his childhood. I was thrilled to discover a Little Black Sambo book, but after I got to read it once, it went back in a box and I haven't seen it since.

Besides the nursery rhymes and fairy tales, he has some "Big Little Books" from the '40s. These are hard-covered books about four by five inches in size and an inch thick with the story on the left page and a black and white picture on the right. Rog, like most little boys in that era, was a western fan, and some of his books include Red Ryder, Roy Rogers, Gene Autry and the Lone Ranger. Now he is a Louis L'Amour fan and has more than one box full of these westerns that he and my dad shared.

I will confess that during the past few years, Roger had been going through his boxes and eliminating a few things that even he sees no future use for. He had saved entire newspapers when he read things that interested him and he wanted to keep. Now he clips out the item and throws the rest of the paper away.

Former students are occasionally the recipient of some of these clippings, as he has kept news reports of their school activities, graduations, weddings and adult honors. Gradually the basement storage area is becoming slightly more spacious.

Our son-in-law, Steve, has said that one of his fears is that I'll die first and he'll have to help Robin and Randy go through Roger's boxes. Probably a justified fear since Roger's mother lived to be 103 years of age. I know that the grandkids will be up for helping since every once in a while Rog will go through some boxes and have a pile of things he's willing to get rid of and lets them select treasures from his old stuff.

It's always interesting to be privileged to watch him look and sort through his old boxes. We find pictures, toys, old candy, cuff links from some of the many weddings he was in, cards, and things I thought I'd thrown away years ago. Somewhere, in a box hidden clear in back, I know he still has unused Christmas presents from before we were married.

Seriously. He definitely has a trash and treasure gene.

Of course, not all the things Roger thinks he might need again are saved in boxes. For years the pockets of his big winter coats have been a source of amazement. Randy, Robin and I have always known if we need athletic tape, gum, spare change, candy, or an extra glove (he seldom has a matching pair), we can find it in one of Roger's coat pockets.

However, he isn't so eager to throw everything in his coat pockets since he and Steve went to a football game a few years ago. When Roger reached in his pocket for something he pulled out a hot dog left there from the last track season. He assumes he got it at the last cold track meet to eat later, got busy and forgot it was there.

Pandora's Box has nothing on Roger's coat pockets.

FIFTEEN

Where's Waldo?

Most people have heard of Waldo and looked in the books to try to find him in a crowd. In our family, we play "Where's Roger?" In fact, if I'd thought of it, that could have been my first book.

My sister Jeannie suggested we have a Where's Roger? game one cold spring day when many of my extended family journeyed to Grinnell, Iowa, to watch Randy pitch for the Coe College Kohawks. We were all bundled in coats and blankets when out beyond centerfield we saw Roger in his red winter jacket with the hood cinched tightly around his face, walking around looking for a homerun ball.

I tell people that I've spent the majority of my life trying to find my husband, and that's true, although he always says he knows where he is and I shouldn't be so concerned about his whereabouts. I've come to decide that he's right and I shouldn't worry about him like I used to. Now I do consider finding him more of a game than a problem.

When I was growing up, my dad used to say I had "go-itis" because he thought I wanted to go to all the school and social events. When I married Roger, I discovered what being on the go really is. He enjoys a wide variety of things, loves all people and thinks nothing of driving hours to see an event or to visit someone.

As I sit here writing, he is driving three hours to see a former student play basketball and will be back tonight.

After we got married, we attended most of the Jefferson school activities, especially ballgames. Roger would find a seat with me, but would soon be up and visiting someone or walking around.

I specifically remember going to the girls' state basketball tournaments at Vets Auditorium in Des Moines. It was the first winter we were married, and I was excited about attending together. This was in the days of six-on-six, and the place was packed. Our seats were more than half way up in the balcony and past the end of the court, getting near the curtains.

During half time of the first game, Roger said he'd be back and walked down the steps and out into the hallway. I assumed he'd be back for the second half.

I waited.

When he didn't return then or after the end of the game, I began to wonder and worry about his whereabouts. And my feelings were hurt because he hadn't stayed with me. He returned during the second game as if it was no big deal. It took me several years to realize that I could just sit back in my seat and scan the front rows to find him, as he always likes to sit in front so he can see the players up close and feel part of the action.

Since that time it has gotten to be the norm that he will find our seats and then take off to scout out better ones. I just watch him until he finds seats in the front and signals for me to join him. Sometimes he knows someone who gets us good seats. For years we sat close to center court, front row, courtside at the girls' state basketball tournaments.

Friends watching on television often commented on seeing us in the front row beside Senator Grassley in the really good seats. That all ended when the state basketball venue was switched to Wells Fargo Arena, and there was no longer courtside seating.

Not only does Roger like good seating, he likes to be in the know. Many times he's been in places ordinary folks are not supposed to be. He likes to get autographs, so has been known to wander to the team dressing rooms in hopes of catching players as they leave the locker room. If this seemed unlikely, he'd get what he could. Or he will try to get backstage to greet a performer or political candidate. And I'm following along so I don't lose him.

At one state tournament game he had his program autographed by the grandparent of a player.

Not the shy, retiring type, Roger talks to everyone. Because of this he has made tons of friends and is known by everyone. Robin and Steve were just starting out coaching and were amazed at the number of officials and coaches who would ask if she was Roger's daughter or who would go out of their way to come shake his hand when we were at ballgames.

It's a family joke that Roger could talk to a post. Wherever we are, he will find someone to start a conversation with, and since he's such a great guy everyone enjoys talking to him. By the end of the conversation he knows where they're from, why they are at that specific event and has made a connection with someone they both know.

SIXTEEN

Kum & Go Ties / This Old Hat

Roger always dressed up for school, church and anywhere else we would go.

Everyone was always impressed that he looked so professional and wore a tie. What they didn't know was that during cold weather he wore the tie to help keep warm. He always enjoyed having a new tie and would give a pop to the first student who commented on his wardrobe addition. Teaching in the middle school let him have some fun with the ties and he had ties for most holidays, Hawkeye ties, cartoon ties, sports ties, political ties and any other unique ones we'd found.

Of course, with this interest in ties, he notices other people's and comments on them. Most mornings, since we've been retired, one or both of us goes into Kum & Go gas station to get our morning cappuccino. Roger had evidently commented many times on the ties that the employees wear there. Now he has some of their old ties with different kinds of candy, sodas and other advertisement on them. Being retired has relaxed Roger's dress code, and about the only time he wears a tie is to church, and a Snickers or Mountain Dew tie doesn't seem appropriate.

Sometimes his choice of shirt, pants and tie for school was questionable. I was glad to see the era of plaid pants end, so patterns were one less thing for him to think about.

As Robin got older, she became our fashion consultant, which was great. He would take suggestions from her better than he would from me. However, sometimes he thought we were too picky, and in his stubbornness he would wear whatever he selected. I remember one day when Robin said she thought we should pin a note on his shirt that said "I dressed myself."

He went to school but we all had a good laugh when the middle school secretary called and commented that, "Roger had an interesting combination on today."

The article of clothing that Roger will best be remembered for is his hat. His all-time favorite is a Bear Bryant-style hat. If you remember this famous football coach, I'm sure you can picture the hat I'm talking about.

Roger did look very dapper in it—when it was new. I don't remember when he got the hat, but it had to be when our kids were little. Each year as the weather got colder, out would come the hat. Since it was comfortable and warm, he wore it to ballgames, church and socializing. In other words, he wore it all the time.

As years went by it was sat on, stepped on, dropped under bleachers and had become a source of fun for all the grandkids as they tried it on, sat on it and hid it from Grandpa. Many was the time that it seemed to be lost. Each time he left it somewhere, even out of town, someone would find it and return it. No one else had a hat like it so it was easily identified.

Roger really didn't want to give it up, but understood that it wasn't in the best of shape. So we started the search for another hat. But it had to be just like the old one. Tough assignment.

None of the stores in Des Moines had anything that he thought was comparable. I bought him a couple of not-so-cheap hats from highly regarded men's stores. Rog would wear them a couple times and tell me they just weren't what he wanted.

When we went to Florida, we looked for hats and even checked out places around Alabama where he thought Bear got his hat. Nothing.

One night we arrived home to find a plastic bag on our front doorknob. Inside was a hat with no note or indication of who had left it. It was the right style and size, a different color but still plaid. It took him a while to get used to it, but he decided if someone who knew him thought he needed a new hat, he probably did.

A couple weeks later, a friend asked if Rog had found the hat he'd left for him.

Now that black and grey plaid hat is the one worn all the time, and it looks so much better than the old blue plaid hat. If fact, the original hat isn't anywhere to be seen in the house. I'm sure it's being saved in a box somewhere.

SEVENTEEN

It's a Secret

Roger tries to keep it under wraps, but everyone knows what a good guy he is. For example, for many years during the cold weather months he would open the middle school gym for students to come in before school and shoot baskets in the gym. As a coach he was hoping to improve the students' skills, but he also was giving them a chance to have fun with friends and let off some steam before settling down for classes.

After our retirement he found that none of the remaining faculty members took it upon themselves to continue this practice. He missed the interaction with the students, so got permission to continue that activity three times a week from November first until May first. It's just a short time, but the middle school students look forward to it.

We did get a good laugh when he substituted in a classroom one day and was surprised that some of the students didn't know his name. One boy said, "We just call you Mr. Basketball."

Roger is good about volunteering his services for various activities but that quite often means that I end up helping him. Latest case in point was when he convinced the session at church that we needed to have a garage sale to clean out items the church no longer needed. This time he ended up with the entire congregation involved as almost everyone cleaned out their house to add to the sale. As he talked to more people, the day ended up including a bake sale, coffee shop, May basket sale and an annex at a church member's barn. All for a good cause and everyone working had fun.

Quite often, while still teaching and coaching, Roger would take on more than he could do, and I would end up making political calls or doing something else he had promised would get done. However, I usually got a surprise for helping. The first time this happened, I was rewarded for my hard work for a political fund-raiser by getting flowers from Governor Robert D. Ray. I was a little taken back until I realized Roger had signed the card.

This was all in good fun, and after a while I didn't even question it when getting cards or flowers from famous people. In the days before cell phones, when he was gone and wanted to call me, he would call collect and give the operator some fictitious name.

The first time I accepted a collect call from Roger Smith, we weren't even married.

After that, it became standard procedure.

The time that I was really fooled was when I had been in charge of a large school event. It was a big dinner with the high school band and vocal groups performing. Tickets had been sold in advance, every seat was full and there was no extra food, when a parent came in without a ticket, insisting to be seated. She was very vocal and caused stress for all of us while we worked to resolve the problem. Nothing we could do made her happy.

The next day at school I received beautiful flowers with a short apology from her. I was so delighted that she had calmed down and seen that I had done the best I could for her, that when I ran into her daughter in the hallway I gushed about the flowers and told her to thank her mother for me.

Roger thought that was hilarious when I told him about it that evening since, of course, the flowers were from him. I didn't think it was too funny. But I never had trouble with that parent again and Roger made sure that even when he didn't use his name, I'd be in on the joke.

Roger has boundless energy and although his common sense seems lacking, he's very thoughtful. As teachers, we learned to fake it when a former student or parent would visit with us and we didn't know who they were right away. Now I'm no longer shocked when someone thanks me for the nice note or flowers they received from us. Most of the time we will have discussed these things and both know about niceties that the other does, but not always. Either of us could send the note and often people can't tell which of us did it as we both have bad handwriting and people who don't know us well can't tell our handwriting apart.

The most secret of Roger's good deeds took place in the mid-seventies, when we were running the Dairy Queen.

Each day one of his jobs would be to go to the bank and make a deposit from the day before. The bank president happened to be a good friend of ours, and as he and Roger were visiting one day Roger happened to mention that he was going to Des

Moines after leaving the bank. The president asked if he would be willing to do an errand for him while in our capital city. Roger replied that he'd be glad to, but was surprised to find out what he'd just agreed to do.

The friend put some money bags in the trunk of our car and told Roger to deliver them to the parent bank and to bring back the bags he was given in exchange. It must have been common practice for bank personnel to haul the money back and forth, and when Roger was going, it just saved someone else a trip. Rog did the requested errand several times but never did know for sure what he was hauling, as of course he never looked in the trunk to see what was there. Not only did he never look, he never told anyone about these trips carrying who-knows-how-much money.

Quite the adventure, for a mild-mannered school teacher.

EIGHTEEN

The Next Stage—Retirement

Retirement came hard for Roger. First, he's never told anyone but me his age. Years ago we had a pastor who always wanted to know everything about everyone, including their age. Rog balked at this and would list the month and day of his birthday, but not the year. Trying harder to get him to share this information, each year the pastor would invite Roger to the church's Over-Sixty dinner. Roger wasn't sixty and he would mention that to the minister who would continue to invite him every year.

Even when that birthday came, my husband refused to acknowledge it by attending the dinner.

Since sixty is no longer looked upon as old age, and the name offended some people, with the change of pastors this annual dinner was eliminated. Score one for Roger.

When we were first married we somehow talked about retirement, and I had commented that even though he is several years older than I am, I didn't intend to keep working after he retired. I couldn't see myself getting up and going off to work for several years while he had lots of free time and fun. Roger was agreeable and that decision has never been questioned by either of us.

Since I had taken the year off after Robin had the triplets, even though I loved my job, I was never as happy working as I had been before, so I was looking forward to retirement. Roger could have taught school for many more years, but as the grandkids got bigger he knew he was missing out on fun and time playing with them, so that made it a little easier for him to step away.

On a winter day when there was a teachers' in-service, we both turned in our resignations. Since we had free time during the noon hour we went to the local Chinese restaurant for lunch. We were both a bit worried about our decision until we ate our fortune cookies. One said, "God looks after you especially," and the other read, "Your dearest wish will come true."

Thinking that this might be a sign, we decided then to "Let go and let God." Feeling good about moving on to this next stage of our lives we came home and put these fortunes in my Bible, where they remain today.

During these past six years we have continued to support the school and attend sports, plays, music programs, fund-raisers and follow the students. We have been volunteers with the second grade reading program, and Roger has continued to keep the official book for the varsity boys and girls basketball teams, as well as substituting in the middle school. To this day we always are a little taken aback when we drive by and see school in session without us.

One of the most interesting and fun things we have done in retirement is travel Iowa. It was Roger's idea to visit every county and most towns in the state.

We do just a couple days at a time as we leisurely travel the byways, check out all the county courthouses, and each town's churches and antique shops. We travel up and down the streets of the town and eat local. It is truly fun and sometimes more of an adventure than we expected.

In one county seat, Roger went to check out the courthouse while I was at a fabric shop. While he was wandering through, he checked out all the floors so he wouldn't miss anything. He was looking around on the third floor (where the public probably wasn't supposed to be), went into the bathroom. When he came out he saw that down the hall was a big, unfriendly-looking prisoner in orange jumpsuit and shackles. Not seeing anyone else around, he decided to make a quick escape—Roger, not the prisoner.

He was really glad to get out of there. Usually he had me take his picture in front of the county courthouses. We have given up that idea as we never wrote down which he was in front of and if it didn't have a visible county sign, by the time he got the pictures printed we'd forgotten which county we were in.

On the journey around Iowa we followed part of the Mormon Trail and saw remnants of towns founded along the way, cemeteries and markers logging the progress of the large number of Mormons as they moved west.

One day we saw several signs about a house to visit. Neither of us had ever heard of it, but since we were not on a time schedule we decided to follow the signs and see where they led. As we turned on to a gravel road and drove through a farmstead, I was ready to turn back, but Roger was curious.

The house turned out to be a place that had once been part of the Underground Railroad and had fascinating information about the family that had once lived there, and where and how the slaves were hidden and kept safe until they could travel on north.

Other days we found ourselves in Amish areas. We enjoyed sharing the roads with their buggies, visiting quilt, basket and furniture shops, seeing Amish children play outside their school at recess time and shopping in the old-fashioned country stores.

Sometimes we traveled farther, to Georgia and Florida to see Randy and our beloved grandson, Trent.

Often we flew, but one of our favorite trips was when we drove and had decided ahead of time that this would include sightseeing instead of the usually pedal-to-the-metal, drive-it-in-two-days type of trip. Roger wanted to see the state capitals. We especially enjoyed the Mississippi and Louisiana capitals because in the south they seem to work especially hard to make their capitals beautiful.

The visit to the Mississippi capital stands out. Usually when we are traveling, we dress comfortably, and this day was no exception, with Roger attired in jeans and tennis shoes and I wearing a jogging suit.

Upon arriving in Jackson and finding the capital, we hopped out of the car and walked around the grounds. Entering the capital building, we started to get uncomfortable because the legislature was in session and everyone was dressed up. But knowing that we wouldn't know anyone there, we weren't too embarrassed and decided to continue as we were.

The interior was beautiful. As we walked along, several gentlemen in suits stopped their visiting and asked, "How are ya'll today?" and "Can we help ya'll find anything?"

We responded that we were fine and just enjoying visiting their beautiful capitol building, and commented on several especially interesting and lovely things we'd seen. From our response, they could tell we weren't from around the area. After hearing we were visiting from Iowa, they insisted we go to the balcony to watch as the day's session was about to start. We thanked them for the information, headed upstairs and found seats to watch the proceedings.

Shortly after we were seated, a page came and asked our names and where we were from. Thinking this rather strange, we were a bit evasive until he told us that we'd been talking to the speaker of the house and he wanted to introduce us to the legislative group. Being embarrassed, we would rather not have done that, but he was insistent, so we obliged. Sure enough, after they presented a favorite son that had come back from Iraq and a school group that was also visiting, we were asked to stand and be introduced. We received a round of applause and lapel pins for souvenirs.

What an honor for just coming in to visit their capital.

It was on this trip that it was once again pointed out to us how modern our country has become . . . and maybe how untrustworthy. As we ventured farther into the south, the gas stations were not only letting us pay at the pump, but demanding it. Roger hadn't tried using his credit or debit card at the gas pumps, and he wasn't about to start then. He refused to let me use my card because he thought they should trust him to pay, like he always has. Sometimes he would go in and prepay, but some stations wouldn't refund money if he should happen to over-pay, so often we would drive off without getting a full tank of gas.

One station really caused him grief as Rog and the management couldn't come to an agreement on how we could get a full tank of gas. We were in need of the gas as the next town was too far away to risk not getting a full tank, so they struck an agreement. I would have to stand inside by the cashier while Roger filled the tank as assurance that he would not drive off without paying. I was embarrassed and felt like I was being held hostage, but Roger was pleased he could get his gas first and pay inside.

Being on the road more than the average person, it's amazing that Roger hasn't been stopped for traffic violations very often. When we bought our most recent car, we did it just the day before we were to leave on a driving trip to Florida, and we didn't notice that the windows were tinted rather dark.

Many times in life it's who you know that makes a difference, and so it was after we got home when Rog was stopped by an Iowa highway patrolman who pointed out the darkness of the windows. Fortunately, this particular patrolman happened to be a former student who just told him to get the tint removed from the front windows before they met again or the next time he would get a ticket.

Roger most recently ran afoul of the law when we were returning from a rural graduation party several miles outside a nearby town. Before heading home for an evening church service, we drove toward the neighboring town to check if gas there was indeed fifteen cents a gallon cheaper than in Jefferson. We must have been in an interesting discussion as Rog wasn't paying attention to his speed and when we met the local deputy, Roger was going more than ten miles an hour over the limit.

Without even checking the rearview mirror for flashing lights, he knew he would be stopped. He pulled over and the officer came to our car to say that he'd clocked him ten miles an hour over the limit. He then asked where we were going in such a hurry, to which Roger answered, "We just left a graduation and need to be in Jefferson in church in ten minutes."

The officer asked to see Roger's driver's license, vehicle registration and proof of insurance. As Roger got out his license, we both knew he was busted as he doesn't think people should have to carry the registration and proof of insurance in the car. We obediently checked the glove compartment for the requested documents and came up with three out-of-date insurance cards but no registration.

The officer went back to his car to check out our car and Roger's license. When he came back he told Roger that if we met up with a highway patrolman he would probably give him tickets that totaled about $600, but he was letting Rog off with a warning, "Because I don't want God mad at me this weekend."

After that, we knew that no matter what the price of gas, we couldn't stop or the officer would think we weren't really going to church, so we drove past the station where it really was fifteen cents a gallon cheaper.

Now it was after 7 p.m., church had started, we had eight miles to go and there was road construction ahead. The bridge being repaired had one-way traffic with stop lights. Every time we'd come upon this section, from either direction, we'd had a red light. Before we went over the hill, Roger said that if the light was green it would be a sign that we were still to go to church, even though we would be more than twenty minutes late. It was green, so off we went to church.

The next day Roger put the registration and proof of insurance in the glove compartment.

~ ~ ~

It's said that learning new things keeps your mind sharp, so Roger decided to add household repair to his repertoire. Although his father was good at this, he'd never taught this son those skills, so I usually didn't allow Roger to use tools in the house.

However, when he decided to put up a new towel bar in the bathroom, I didn't see how that could go wrong and wanted to be supportive, so he purchased the bar and went to work. He carefully measured and followed the directions, but it didn't work. The directions were for an eighteen-inch bar and he'd bought a twenty-four-inch one so the bar didn't fit between the holders.

Roger did a great job the second time, the towel bar fit, it was strong. but we still had the other holes in the wall. The tools went back outside.

After being retired for several years, we discussed how a larger kitchen would be helpful since I love to cook and like to take food to others, especially Robin's family.

Since we had added onto the house twice already, one day Roger said, "Well, we could just build a new house." I was all over that idea and soon we enlisted the instructor for the local high school construction class to make our new house the project for the following year.

Roger had few things that he wanted in the plan. His main interest was his future den. He wanted it computer-free, with a large closet for more boxes and a window so he could see across the street to know when the neighbor was outside mowing. With the help of a friend and relative, the plans were made and in the fall construction started.

The construction was exciting, and because the new home was being built about one hundred yards behind where we lived, we checked on it often or were called back to okay or decide different things.

Again, Roger didn't want to be involved in too many of the decisions but was adamant about some things he wanted. Mostly, he just enjoyed going out and helping sweep up at the end of the day.

The next May, when it was finished, the school construction class had an open house. Randy and Steve helped move furniture, Robin helped unpack and the interior design class helped stage the house.

It was a fun evening, and after everyone left we and our family spent our first night in the house.

While getting ready for the open house, everyone had cleaned up in the old house, but now that we were living in our new abode, the bathrooms were no longer off limits. However, Roger had trouble adjusting. Change can be hard, so for at least two weeks he would wander up to the old house for his shower.

Moving to somewhere close can have its advantages, but it can make it harder to finish the job and get everything moved out. In the couple of months that took, the housing market tanked, so we still own two houses.

Rog also didn't change the address for our newspaper delivery so we continued to get the paper at the door of the other house each morning for several weeks. It was several months later when the local post office told us we would have to get a new mailbox and get our address changed on everything.

Now, after three years in our new home, we are both happy with our decision and have adjusted well. Roger wasn't in favor of a sunroom and for the first year didn't venture out there. Now he occasionally uses it and has heard enough people admire it that I hope he thinks it's a good addition.

Once he became accustomed to the house, everything has gone well with the exception of our bedroom. The second Christmas here we were on the garden club's tour of homes. One of my friends thought our bedroom would show off better if we moved the bed at an angle. Rog knew he wouldn't like it and wouldn't help rearrange it to the new angle.

The room looked great, but Roger had trouble sleeping because he said it was hard to sleep crooked.

~ ~ ~

We had always had real Christmas trees before moving, but since Randy and Robin had long ago moved out of the house, we no longer felt the desire to put up a real tree. Perhaps Roger's tendency to purchase trees with crooked trunks was part of the problem. While our kids were still home, they and Roger would go to a local tree farm, select a tree, saw it down and bring it home. Our marriage worked better if I then left the house for at least an hour while they attempted to get the tree to stand up straight. I tended to become very agitated when Roger would pound nails into the walls so he could tie the tree to the wall to prevent it falling over.

Knowing that putting up a Christmas tree usually stressed us both out, some years he would put it off until too close to the date to suit me. One year we were especially late selecting a tree and came home to find one the height we usually selected leaning against our front door. With it was a note from the owner of the tree farm saying it was getting close to Christmas and since we hadn't been out, he selected one for us with a crooked trunk since he remembered Roger always picked out that kind.

Being really big spenders, we purchased two fake trees for a total of $20 from friends who were moving away. Now we are saving money and stress each Christmas season so we really can have a merry holiday—and no nail holes in the walls.

NINETEEN

If I Had Known

I never understood when my Dad would say, "If I'd known having grandkids was this much fun, I would have had them first," but he was right.

When we had Randy and Robin, we were so busy trying to make a living that we didn't always enjoy them as much as we should have. When Randy's son, Trenton, was born, Roger said, "It's kind of like we get another chance."

Being grandparents is the best part of getting older and retirement has made it possible to enjoy them even more. When we were kids we thought our grandparents were really old. As adult health has changed through the years, grandparenting has also and we are lucky to feel young enough to wrestle, play ball and do other activities short of racing them. Becoming a grandpa didn't bother Roger as much as the realization that now he would be sleeping with a grandma.

What excitement there was when Trent was born. As soon as Randy called with the good news, we started checking airlines for flights to Florida and arrived to see him when he was three days old. We stayed for a week and spent our time feeding and rocking him, reading to him and just watching him sleep. Knowing that we would miss many milestones in his life because of the distance we lived apart, we vowed to make sure we saw him at least twice a year.

One of the most exciting things to ever happen to us was when Robin and Steve announced they would be the parents of triplets. We'd been praying for a baby to add to their family but everyone was surprised to get three at once. What a blessing. All of us are continually thankful for the addition of Nolan, Summer and Kaleb, and the fact that all were physically and mentally well.

Three and a half years later they added Kameron to the clan, and the family was complete.

For Roger, having grandchildren was like having new playmates. He got down on the floor and lay with them, just looking at them and talking, when they were babies.

As they've gotten older, he's just enjoyed each stage, but having them follow him around and learn to like some of his favorite activities has been the best.

The importance of early education is well known, so as Randy and Robin were mentored by grandparents, friends and neighbors as well as by us, we got to do the same for our grandchildren. With everyone blessed with different talents, children have a wide variety of educators. As a math teacher, Roger has passed on a skill with numbers. The grandchildren have had fun learning different games with Grandpa O.

For young Kameron he made up a game called red and black. She could choose either color, and when he would deal out the cards, there was almost always more of her color than his.

Kameron has now advanced to real games.

Starting when the grandkids were just learning their numbers, playing cards with Grandpa has been a favorite activity. They were doing addition and subtraction at early ages and by age eight all have been good at doing math in their heads with numbers much larger than in their card games. Beating Grandpa is always the goal.

Of course Roger is helping them with sports. The only time he's felt like he really didn't know what was going on was when Robin enlisted his help coaching the triplets' soccer team when they were four. Fortunately the main skill they need to know is how to kick, and the main direction needed for four-year-olds is which way to the goal.

The coaches could handle that. Now that they are eight, that sport is best left to others to coach so we can watch and still learn.

All of our grandchildren are town kids, so the most fun they have with Grandpa is outdoors, sledding, having snowball fights and tromping in the woods behind our house. It has been Roger's desire to make a cute playhouse for them, but with his lack of carpentry skills the hideouts have been made from used lumber, crudely put together. But the kids love it, so that's what counts.

For years he has had the kids following him around and learning a variety of skills. They have always loved to help rake, plant gardens, pick up sticks and any other thing Grandpa was doing. Just recently, after having the grandkids help haul junk to the dump, fix the sheep pen and do some work at church, he confided in me that, "Now that the kids are older, I can really get a lot of work done while they're here."

Meanwhile, one of the triplets told their mom that "Grandpa doesn't think we know he has us doing work, but it's okay because we like to help him."

It must be the trips to the donut shop, playing Frisbee golf in the yard, and all the card and board games that make the work worthwhile.

Just like when our children were young, we try to make it to most of their school and church programs as well as sporting events. Robin will be quick to say Roger never went to her swim meets. But he goes to watch the grandkids swim and has even gone to dance recitals. It's all worth it when one of them sits on his lap.

It's only a matter of time before they know more than we do. Now even the five-year-old can program our phones and run the television and computers better than we can.

TWENTY

Happily Ever After

Before the aforementioned tour of homes, I hung some wall sayings around the house.

My favorite is in our bedroom: "It doesn't matter where you go in life . . . it's who you have beside you that makes it worthwhile."

That couldn't be more true. I suppose that I could have married someone else and been happy, but I can't believe my life would have been as much fun. Before we were married, Roger told me we'd never be rich and we never have been in dollars. But in the things that matter, we've been blessed. It is so much fun to have a mate for life that makes each day an adventure. Truly.

The list of funny/absentminded things Roger has done could go on and on—like how he tried to sell Robin and Steve's wedding napkins at a garage sale, even though they had their names and the date on them. And just last night he wore two different-colored tennis shoes to a ballgame. He recently dubbed us the Hartley Hillbillies as we drove his little pickup a couple of hours with a mattress and box springs tied down. (In our defense, they were new and we didn't have any pots and pans hanging out the side.)

We still have to explain common sense things to him, such as the comics, and how to work the grandkids' toys. But, more important, the good he has done could fill another book.

He always does the deep cleaning and washes the windows for me, is generous to our children and grandchildren with time and resources, and is well respected in the community for his years of dedication to children and volunteering.

My younger sister, who has always had a way with words, sent me this note recently about a time years ago when he stepped up and made a difference in her life.

> *Reading your Roger stories reminded me of a time he was my white knight, and I keep forgetting to tell you. I just wanted to remind you what a prince I think he is. When Matthew was in about seventh grade, playing summer baseball, Butch Fenn was his coach. One evening Judy Fenn called me and said at the end of every season, Butch always had the boys play a father-son game. He had announced this a couple of times and asked who would be there, and every time Matthew looked away and didn't indicate he would be there.*
>
> *Butch felt badly about it and he and Judy thought maybe I could work something out.*
>
> *I wanted to cry, but asked Matthew about it later and he said no, he didn't want to go and feel dumb without a dad. Grandpa covered for him at 4-H functions and school, but he couldn't play baseball and Matt just didn't want to go, and he didn't want to tell me 'cuz he knew I would feel bad. I asked him if he wanted to try to find his dad; we often had no idea where he*

was but once in a while he would show up in Des Moines. No, he didn't want his dad to come.

I was desperate, the game was in four days and I couldn't think. I suggested Uncle Monty but Matt said no, he plays at all the girls games for them. Then Roger came to mind. I went to the phone and dialed your number, and Roger answered. I asked him to please, please come and do this for Matt. He hesitated just a minute, I'm sure he already had committed to something, but then he said sure, he would be glad to. When I told Matthew, he jumped up and down and said "Really? He'll come? He knows how to play ball and everything!" He was beyond thrilled. I called Butch and Judy, thanked them and said Matthew would be playing with Roger.

The night of the game, Roger showed up to play with his own glove (several of the dads had to borrow one) which won points with Matthew right away. First time in field, Roger caught a pop fly and made an out, then at bat he got on second base. Matthew was walking on air and kept looking at me in the stands and grinning. When they would switch and go out to bat, Roger would high-five Matthew and kid him about being beaten by old guys.

I know we both thanked Roger several times, but it meant so much to us. Matthew has always referred to Roger as a "stand up guy," and I know he helped him know at an early age that some guys take off, but many stand up and show up when they are needed.

Kleenex anyone?

Our eight-year-old grandson, Nolan, was to write about someone he admired (I'm not really sure what the assignment was) and he did the best job of describing his grandpa.

Grandpa O

Grandpa O likes sports like me his favorite football team is the Iowa Hawkeyes.

His faborite baseball team is the Minnesota Twins. He coaches girls track.

He is a very nice man. He goes to church and reads his bible. He also loves god!!! He tells me lots of stories of when he was a little kid. He also has a penny collection it is very cool. He has a phone and computer but he does not know how to work them so we have to teach him. He has gone to many places to help people after hurcanes, tornadoes, and storms he is a math teacher for 7th grade. He has a ping pong table that is fun. He bilt us a fort outside that our grandma does not no adout. He has gone to a lot of Iowa *games. When I grow up I want to be like my grandpa!!!!!*

Need I say more?

THE END

ORDER FORM

Mail Order Form To: Rosemarie Olhausen
                      1409 West Lincolnway
                      Jefferson, IA 50129

My Life with Roger:
   Celebrating Forty-Plus Years of Laughter,
   Travel and Sports
ISBN: 978-0-9833526-4-8

$14.00 ea
.98 sales tax ea

S&H per quantity: $3.00 for 1 – 3 books

Enclosed is check or money order for: $_____

Payable to Rosemarie Olhausen

NAME: _____

ADDRESS:_____

_____

Other Titles by Shapato Publishing:

The Earth Abides
    Betty Taylor

Good Fences
    Marshall Crane

Life with My Wife: The Memoir of an Imperfect Man
    Roger Stoner

Red & the Wolfe: A Lake Okoboji Fable
    Jean Tennant

God's Hand in a Foreign Land
    Nancy Evanson

The Island Calls: A True-Life Novel about a Chamorro Daughter Finding Her Way Back Home
    Teresa Garrido Roberts

Walking Beans Wasn't Something You Did With Your Dog: Stories of Growing Up in and Around Small Towns in the Midwest
    Edited by Jean Tennant

Knee High by the Fourth of July: More Stories of Growing Up in and Around Small Towns in the Midwest
    Edited by Jean Tennant

Amber Waves of Grain: Third in the Series of Stories about Growing Up in and Around Small Towns in the Midwest
    Edited by Jean Tennant

Made in the USA
Charleston, SC
05 November 2011